GET HIRED!

Winning Strategies to Ace the Interview

REVISED EDITION

PRAISE FOR
GET HIRED!

"*If you Google the Internet for 'behavioral interviewing,' you will get 1,400,000 results. But Paul Green is not just another writer on this subject—he is the very inventor of the term. In* **Get Hired!** *(2006 Revised Edition), he updates his 1996 classic with new and original thinking that I, personally, found fascinating. I admire it greatly. It will certainly change the way I think, and talk, about finding a job. I think it will for you, too.*"

Richard Nelson Bolles

Author, *What Color Is Your Parachute? 2006*
The best-selling job hunting book in the world

"*The coach's tips are very helpful—advice from a pro. Paul's book will help you spot trouble areas that you can fix or avoid and help you focus on what you have to offer to land the job.*"

Marjorie Blanchard, Ph.D.

"*Paul Green is one of the world's leading experts on interviewing. Packed with great content, his new book is worth far more than the price. Everyone would be a big winner if companies would give a copy to all their job candidates.*"

Arthur R. Bauer

Founder, American Media Inc.

GET HIRED!

Winning Strategies to Ace the Interview

REVISED EDITION

Paul C. Green, Ph.D.

SKILFAST INC.

GET HIRED!
Winning Strategies to Ace the Interview

SkilFast® Inc.
516 Tennessee Street, Suite #125
Memphis, TN 38103-4717
Phone (toll free) 866-579-3942   Fax 901-312-8854

Ordering Information

To order additional copies, contact National Book Network at 800-462-6420 or **nbnbooks.com**, or contact your local bookseller. Quantity discounts are available.

For more information or to contact the author, visit our website at **paulcgreenphd.com**.

ISBN 0-9771414-1-1 cloth
ISBN 0-9771414-0-3 paperback

Library of Congress Cataloging-in-Publication Data

Green, Paul C.
      Get hired; winning strategies to ace the interview / Paul C. Green
        p.   cm.
      Library of Congress Control Number 2005906449
      Includes bibliographical references and index.
      ISBN 0-9771414-1-1. — ISBN 0-9771414-0-3 (pbk.)
      1. Employment interviewing—Handbooks, manuals, etc. 2. Job Hunting – Handbooks, manuals, etc. I. Title

---

Credits

Managing editor: Jeff Morris
Proofreaders: Deborah Costenbader, Bobbie Jo Sims
Index: Linda Webster
Cover and text design: Jeff Morris
Cover photography: Marshall Harrington Photography

First Edition
First printing: May 1996
Second printing: October 1996

Revised Edition
First printing: February 2006

To my brother

Phil Cox Green

who taught me words

nudged me toward college

teaches patiently

models integrity

loves unconditionally

and shapes happy thoughts

CONTENTS

ABOUT THE AUTHOR

Paul Green is an industrial organizational psychologist with over thirty-five years of experience in consulting, nationally and internationally. His primary area of professional practice was in assessing job candidates and coaching managers in how to conduct a job search. Using both tests and interviews, he conducted 5,000 interviews on candidates for a broad range of positions. He converted this practice into Behavioral Technology, Inc., a management training company that merged with six other training firms into Provant, which was traded as "PROVANT" on the New York Stock Exchange.

Paul coined the term "behavioral interviewing" and developed an interview training seminar that has been attended by several hundred thousand managers worldwide. His interviewing approach is used by an estimated 40 percent of employers in the United States. His interviewing techniques were adapted into a video production, *More Than a Gut Feeling*, which was recognized by *FORTUNE* magazine as being one of the all-time bestselling training films in any category. His understanding of the selection process is the foundation for the current revision of *Get Hired!*

Paul welcomes questions and comments. Feel free to contact him at paulcgreen@skilfast.com.

ABOUT THE REVISED *GET HIRED!*

Get Hired! was first published in 1996. At that time Monster.com was a startup company, candidates did mass mailings of thousands of résumés, economic growth seemed to have an endless horizon, and employers were confident in their business models. Now things are different.

The Internet is a major tool in a job search, from the perspective of sourcing leads, posting your résumé, and reviewing employer literature. Paper résumés are hardly the tool they once were, and telephone or Internet video interviews will be the next big trend. Accordingly, I removed sections talking about résumés and expanded the "how to" of not being face-to-face.

Another change seems to have occurred with employers. Not only are there threats from terrorism, but the news is full of corporate accounting scandals, rising employment costs, and shareholder revolts. We are in an uncertain business environment that will last for some unknown time. This led me to recast much of the book into ways to make your interviewer feel secure in making you an offer. You need to show how you are over the line, not borderline.

The competency movement in human resources has been woven into the day-to-day fabric of employment. Now the self-assessment in chapter 5 involves developing a competency profile that suggests the types of skills you should emphasize in the interview. The new Comp-A-Lizer will help you with this and make *Get Hired!* even more at your service in preparing for interviews.

Several things have not changed. It remains important to prepare to take behavior-based interviews with past event questions organized under competencies. One survey showed that about 40 percent of Fortune 1000 companies now use the technique. Testing of job candidates continues to be a standard practice for jobs with a high public impact or with critical performance demands. And it seems that the marketplace continues to be hungry for your skills. Employers want to know, "What can you do for me now?" You need to be prepared to answer.

Regardless of how structured or efficient interviewing becomes, the human side of the interview continues. Candidates are real people with goals, fears, and responsibilities. They take interviews from interviewers who also are real people and who are often unsure and poorly trained. This sets the challenge for me as your author—I want to help you get hired with dignity by being honest and helpful, even with interviewers who aren't at their best. For you, the challenge is to prepare and practice—then things will work out just fine.

Paul C. Green, Ph.D.
Memphis, February 2006

ACKNOWLEDGMENTS

This new edition of *Get Hired!* is the product of the skill and commitment of many people.

First, there are the many people who bought the first book and actually communicated with me. Generally this was about thanking me for helping them advance their careers. But sometimes it was a complaint that I didn't do such-and-such. All of this was appreciated and incorporated into the writing of this book. Being a writer puts one in solitude. It's like having a one-way conversation with imaginary people. Those who communicated with me made the targets of my writing more personal and real.

Ray Bard is the owner of Bard Press, the original publisher of *Get Hired!* Along every step of the way, he was a source of encouragement and support. After the book was published, he continued to give me guidance on marketing, book tours, and the "how to" of the book business. When book sales slowed in the fall of 2002, Ray was an icon of integrity as we struggled with the challenges of a slow market. Because of all these actions, Ray Bard is a living behavioral model for how to make a book financially, as well as personally, profitable.

Jeff Morris was the editor on the first and second versions of the book. He has been a twenty-four-hour source of professional experience and personal support. On the first version he was tenacious on maintaining the book's vision in every chapter, every section, every word. Sometimes we irritated each other, sometimes we postponed conclusions, sometimes we fought, but always we respected each other's role in the process. Jeff proved himself again with this project. Operating on a shoestring, he edited, designed, composed, and guided me around the obstacles.

I did a book tour when the original version of *Get Hired!* was published. The people at Planned Television Arts in New York City were very helpful. They set me up with a total of ninety-nine events, including broadcast media appearances and book signings. I learned a lot from them on how to get the message across. I also learned from the call-ins who grilled me on national television and radio. This experience was about more than book marketing. Books have an impact on people. Authors need to do a good job. I take this very seriously.

Thank you all.

RECOGNIZE OPPORTUNITY

Some time ago I got a telephone call from a friend who was very troubled. Now, this is someone I once worked with and have known for years. He was, and still is, a rock-solid guy. In all the time I worked with him I never saw him rattled, even when he was being yelled at by his boss. But on this day his speech was halting and his voice was shaking. He had just been terminated.

"I got sideways between my boss and the VP of operations," he said. "Not the first time, as you well know, but this time it went against me. I was right, but career-wise I was dead wrong. They didn't fire me right away; they waited a decent interval, then 'downsized' my position. So I'm on the street now, a place I never thought I'd be at my age.

"Fact is, Paul, I don't know what to do. You have helped hundreds with their careers, but I don't think I've got much of a chance. The competition's going to be murder. I'll have to go up against people who still have jobs, and what organization's going to choose a guy my age who's been cut loose?"

It was a story I've heard many times before and many times since—though never from someone I knew so well. I was glad he had called me; I knew I could help.

"I know it feels like it's the end of the world and you're the last person left alive," I told him, "but believe me—you're not alone. The whole world of work is turning upside down. Everybody's changing jobs, and everybody's job is changing. You'd be surprised at how many people are having the same experience."

17

I told him—and I'm telling you now—that the job market is changing at breakneck speed. That's your real competition. You are competing against change. Everyone else has the same challenge. In fact, you may have a distinct advantage over other people doing a job search. I'll tell you why.

You already know that the employment situation is a moving target, in constant flux. But what's not so obvious is that so much change makes organizations "risk averse." In the big picture they are concerned about accounting scandals, shareholder revolts, terrorism, and lawsuits. By the time they start to think about hiring, they want to feel secure that you can both pay your way and get profitable results. A lot of emotional energy has been depleted by the time you show up for your interview.

Employers try hard not to hire people. To keep from hiring, they drag their feet on creating jobs, outsource labor offshore, and use technology. Instead of facing the personal and financial costs of terminating a real person, organizations want to be able to unplug a resource. They want to stay lean and profitable, in case there's a downturn.

For you, this means the tables have turned. Just a few short years ago it was the job seekers who were insecure; today, it's the interviewers. But this makes your task clear: you must show the interviewer that you will be a rock-solid, exceptional hire. If the interviewer feels confident that hiring you will bring profitable results, you are more likely to get an offer. To create this feeling, you have to learn how to describe your skills in a professional, respectful way: no bragging, no put-downs, just an honest description of what you can do the day you show up for work.

Preparation means taking the right steps to recognize your skills and share them with an employer. I will volunteer to be your job coach throughout this book. Together, we will determine exactly what skills you need to highlight in your interviews. You will learn how to convert bad feelings into positive energy, say the right thing on the telephone, cultivate advocates, give a smooth review of your career, make skill-benefit statements, share examples of how you have used your skills, and respond to killer questions with dynamite answers. When you are ready, doors will open for you.

It's hard work, but that's okay. After all, when you take the right steps with discipline, it's likely that you will Get Hired!

1

SETTING OUT ON YOUR JOB JOURNEY

Because you've opened this book and started reading, I can tell you something about yourself that is probably true:

You're looking for a job.

Maybe you lost your last position in a corporate restructuring. Maybe you have a job now but you're thinking of leaving it, or you're worried about losing it. Maybe you've been out of the job market for a while and want to get back into it. Maybe you're a high school or college graduate looking for your first job. Or maybe your organization is downsizing and you've been asked to interview in order to keep the job you now have.

Whatever your situation, you're probably feeling the stress. One day you're full of courage and optimism, moving inexorably onward and upward toward your career destiny; the next day you're down, worried that you won't get the interview you want, or that the interviewer won't like you, or that you'll blow it and lose your chance at your dream job.

Don't worry—these ups and downs are perfectly normal. A lot of it has to do with the culture we live in—a culture that places enormous value on employment, in which a person's self-esteem, rightly or wrongly, is tied closely to working and being paid for it. When you're out of a job, your self-esteem may start to fall, and if you're unemployed for long, it can plummet out of sight and make it that much harder to get out and look for work.

I will offer two practical tips about coping with your feelings. First, it's not a disgrace to be out of a job. It's a very common experience these days. The workplace is changing rapidly, and people change jobs more often than they used to. Second, the best way to regain and sustain your confidence and self-esteem is to take action. Action combats anxiety.

You've already taken the first positive step toward correcting your situation: you've started reading this book. If you follow its advice, you will dramatically increase your chances of getting a good job—the job that you're suited for, perhaps even the dream job you've been steering your career toward.

This book will help you learn how to

- manage your feelings in and around interviews,

- provide specific, honest information about your skills,

- talk about how the employer can benefit by hiring you,

- respond to questions about negatives in your skills,

- keep your mouth shut on potentially explosive issues,

- pick up the pieces when you don't get the job offer,

and much more. Along the way I will share with you my years of experience interviewing candidates for a wide variety of jobs in both the private sector and government. I will give you practical advice based on over ten years of experience as an outplacement consultant, helping people find new jobs. From my experience in training tens of thousands of managers how to conduct selection interviews, I will explain what you can expect most interviewers to say and do.

WHAT IT'S ALL ABOUT

The focus of *Get Hired!* is the interview. In writing the book, I tried to put myself in your shoes—a job candidate aspiring to do well enough in an interview to get a job offer.

The four parts of the book will tell you, in turn, how to recognize opportunities in today's job market, how to prepare for your interviews with confidence, how to get interviews and what to say in them, and how to move ahead after every interview. I wrote the book with an image of you in mind—full of feelings, facing change, open to adventure—and the idea of building a relationship between us that will make this book a friendly reference for you to use throughout your career.

Rather than making *Get Hired!* a series of prescriptions for answering specific questions, I have chosen to help you understand the skills and competencies you have to offer and as well as use your self-assessment to develop an honest, effective answer to any question you are asked. If you spend enough time planning and practicing these techniques for answering questions, you'll be able to talk about the real you without sounding canned.

I've seen over the years how a flawed selection process often yields poor matches between the tasks that need to be done and the people hired to do them. Both candidates and organizations suffer as a result. Then there are stereotypes and prejudice. I've watched unqualified job seekers finesse their way into a job and seen excellent candidates let themselves fall victim to the biases of poorly trained interviewers. I've also been witness to the happy results of a careful, rational, unbiased selection process. This book translates these beliefs and experiences into the actions you need to take in order to improve your interviewing effectiveness.

I encourage you to take action in another way as well. If you own this book, use it. Write in it; underline important ideas; do the exercises; make graphs and drawings; dog-ear key pages; scribble in the margins or in the spaces provided, like the one you see here. This is the starting point for being truly involved in the process of interview preparation. Now, if this book is borrowed

---

Thoughts:

or on loan from a library, don't mark a single page—use a note pad. But here's the reality: when you respond, your learning will be several hundred times more valuable than the cost of the book. If you are a passive reader, you'll get less out of it.

NEW WAYS OF WORKING

I've also seen how the accelerating pace of change has overtaken the job market over the last few years. Change is the only thing you can be sure of now. Everything about a job that you had once, have now, or want to have, is changing. The dream career you planned five years ago has probably evaporated.

The forces driving this transformation are many and complex. Technological changes and global competition are two of the most obvious. To survive in this climate, organizations must service demanding customers. Employees must get more done in less time. Self-directed work teams take the place of individual jobs. Moreover, the application of new technologies and self-management is making traditional managers an endangered species. The new standard is "more, better, faster."

The traditional concept of the job is becoming a relic of the past, at least in large corporations. If you're interviewing for a newly created job, chances are that the organization hasn't had the time to write a job description. Even if you stay in your current job, in three years the work you're doing will probably be different. If you're reading this book to prepare for a promotional interview, the odds are that the job you want will change as well. On the bright side, if you hate your current job, the odds are that it, too, will change. These clouds have silver linings.

NEW WAYS OF HIRING

There is a lot of variation in the way interviews are done. You can expect some interviews to be informal conversations, whereas others will use a structured approach with prepared questions. Some will focus on your ability to be a good fit with the culture; others will deal with your competencies and technical knowledge. The questions will range from hypothetical, or "situational," questions to past-event, or "behavioral," questions. You may take the interview with one person, a series of people, or several people all at once. The interview may be administered face-to-face, over the telephone, or through the Internet. The options seem endless.

Each organization will have its own style of interviewing, usually a combination of different techniques. It's hard for you to know what to expect. Will the interview be a friendly chat with a sympathetic listener, or a grilling by a gang of flinty-eyed interrogators? Will there be personal questions? Will your answers be scored, or will the interviewer base his decision on his general impression of you?

As you will see, not knowing what sort of interview you will encounter doesn't have to hurt your chances. If you prepare for a behavior-based interview, you will be most likely to present the best case for yourself with any kind of interview. You will communicate your job-related skills honestly and effectively, and you will help the interviewer base the hiring decision on a reasonable prediction of how well you will do the job.

In fact, preparing for the behavior-based interview highlights your strengths in any type of selection process—new hires, promotions, internal placement. It prompts you to discover, rediscover, or examine your own strengths and weaknesses and search for the kinds of jobs you are best suited for. It helps you redefine your skills for your employer. It shows potential new employers how you can contribute to their productivity. Not least, it gives you a positive outlook on the ordeal of looking for employment and helps you keep your dignity in any interview situation, no matter how inept, hostile, or biased the interviewer.

Not everyone finds the job search a totally negative experience. One person told me, "I was devastated at first. It took me completely by surprise. But I soon found that the really important things in life didn't change at all. Something as simple as taking my daughter to Little League gave me the foundation I needed to move on."

Another candidate was delighted to be in her job search. It was an exciting challenge, she said. "After a little bit, I discovered that most interviewers are so bad that just a little bit of preparation would make me do well. When I was ready, I could hold my own with any interviewer."

YOUR PERSONAL JOB COACH

I've been through the job jungle from east to west and north to south, and I've seen it from high and low. My company and its certified trainers conducted thousands of interviewer-training workshops with top-of-the-line organizations having excellent human resource departments that wanted to use an effective and defensible interviewing process. I know how good the interviewing process can be. I've also been able to learn from my own mistakes and those of others, based on what I heard in my classes and outplacement counseling. This book is designed to pass all of these lessons on to you.

Think of me as your personal job coach. Of course, I can't be like your tennis coach or your golf pro, because you are there and I am somewhere else.

Our interaction is limited by the fact that I must speak to you through this book. But I will use these pages to show you how to tap your own natural strengths, your experiences, your personal resources, and some of the outside resources available to you that you may not be aware of. I'll coach you on how to present yourself to make the best impression on those who will decide whether to hire you.

I will encourage you to take an honest, realistic approach to getting a job. If you've interviewed before, you already know that some interviewers can be devious and misleading, encouraging you to blurt out things that can hurt your job chances. Others enjoy wielding power and having the job seeker at their mercy. A good interviewer will treat you fairly and encourage you to make your best case. The techniques outlined in this book will help you deal with the worst interviewers and make the most of the opportunities afforded you by the rest.

DOING YOUR PART

If we were in face-to-face coaching, you would turn to me at times and say, "Yeah, but. . . ." Then I could counter with a more detailed or reasoned explanation of my point. Since I can't defend my ideas to you in person, I'll try throughout this book to anticipate your "yeah-buts" and cover as many of the bases as I can.

YEAH-BUT: My situation is unique. How can you give me advice that will solve my particular problem?

COACH'S COMEBACK: I've talked with more job seekers than you can imagine, and although I don't know your unique situation, I'll bet it's not as unusual as you think. Read on, use what applies to you, and skip the rest.

But much of the responsibility must necessarily fall on you—that is, you must read beyond my words and extend the principles I'm communicating, to work out some of the answers for yourself. Remember, you are the expert on the particular job search you find yourself in. Read the book, analyze the situation, and apply whatever is appropriate. If I were your golf pro, I could tell you which club is best for getting out of the rough a hundred yards from the fourth green. But if you were playing on a strange course in another town, you'd have to remember the general principles I taught you and figure it out for yourself.

Don't let one bad experience with an interviewer, or two, or five, keep you from pursuing your dream job. If they don't hire you, think of it as their loss. It's not your role to help an interviewer rise above his inadequacy. Your task is to get hired, and if you keep moving, you will. Think of me as running alongside you, telling you not to quit.

An in-person coach is also there to spur you on, to defend you from your doubts, to help you to get beyond your "yeah-buts." To some extent, I can do this by anticipating your fears—after all, you wouldn't be the first to let self-doubt hold you back. But you must be the one to push ahead when the going gets rough. Remember this: doing something, taking almost any action, is better than doing nothing. Just visualize me saying to you, "Hey, just do it!" or "Nothing ventured, nothing gained!" or "Seize the day!" You're the job shark. Keep moving to survive.

TAKE COURAGE

As a job seeker, you are starting out on a great journey—one that you may or may not have made before. On this journey you will face challenges both known and unknown. Knowing this, you will probably have some concerns about what you will find.

Fear is not all bad—it is a valuable emotion. Kept under control, it sharpens your perceptions and makes you think more clearly. It will help you prepare to meet the challenges. And I'm here beside you, ready to make the journey with you.

As your personal job coach, my first advice is this: Stay calm, don't worry too much. You're off to a good start. This book is a map of what lies ahead of you. Reading it, understanding it, and using it will greatly increase your chances of getting a good job—a job that you will be well suited for, in an organization that knows and appreciates your strengths and talents.

Thoughts:

Thoughts:

SURF
THE TRENDS

Dreams and opportunities differ in at least one important way. Dreams engage your passion for taking action; opportunities invite you to act on your dreams in a practical way. There's no substitute for discovering interview opportunities that engage your career dreams realistically. But can you realistically expect to find such opportunities in today's uncertain, unstable job market?

The answer is yes. There is much in current workforce trends and projections to both encourage you and guide you in your search for career opportunities. These trends are based on long-term changes in the population and the ongoing technology-driven revolution in work. Regardless how the job market may be at this moment, the trends are always there, carving out niches for you to target in your search.

WATCHING FOR THE RIGHT WAVES

Identifying trends is like watching the surf come in. First, you notice the waves that are hitting the beach. They're pretty obvious. If you're in the water, you feel their power. Sometimes you get knocked down. Next, there are waves a few yards out, the ones that haven't quite broken yet. You see them well in advance, and you can get ready for them.

But the waves you really need to identify are the waves that surfers look for—the subtle swells far from shore, hardly visible, that you need to see early to get a powerful ride. The skilled surfer knows how to identify the good waves, the ones that will take him all the way in and not fizzle halfway to shore.

Just like waves in the surf, some trends don't relate to you or your needs. They're the ones that you don't want to catch. But other trends relate to your job search in general and your interviews in particular. These are the trends that will help you compete in getting hired. These are the waves you need to surf.

TREND NO. 1: THE CHANGING NATURE OF JOBS

Not so long ago it was meaningful to think of getting a job that you could keep for a long time. Trade unions were built around hands-on skills. Administrators were responsible for organization, paperwork, and operational details. Managers built careers in getting other people to do their jobs. We thought in terms of career paths, of progressing through a series of jobs and educational experiences to a well-paid, prestigious, secure position high in some organization's hierarchy.

YEAH-BUT: I know I need to learn new skills, but I'm too old to go back to school!

COACH'S COMEBACK: Maybe you don't really need another degree, but you do need to update your skills constantly. And even if you do have plenty of degrees, they become obsolete if you don't stay current. What skills do employers need today? What will they need in the near future? Read; go online; ask questions; attend seminars. Keep your mind open and your skill base growing. Become your own university.

But this concept of a job has been fading as the pace of change accelerates and more and more segments of the economy are affected. New technologies burst into being, outsourcing moves jobs offshore, old industries die, new organizations are formed to deal with the problems of change. Fewer factory workers are needed—and in these lean, mean times, fewer supervisors, too. Service-based employment multiplies, especially in medical, security, food, and information services.

Instead of being involved in a job search, think of yourself as engaged in a work search. This will make a big difference in the way you approach an interview. When you can identify an employer's needs and match them up with your skills, you may be able to identify work that needs to be done even when no "jobs" are available. Then you can help your potential employer create a job—with yourself as the best candidate for it.

TREND NO. 2: OCCUPATIONAL GROWTH

It may be possible to persuade the interviewer that her organization has an unrecognized need for your skills. But you should be cautious about trying to sell the interviewer on the kind of work you want to do rather than adapting to what the organization needs to have done. You need to be able to list and describe your skills, of course, but stay alert to what the interviewer is asking. Even if the job is in your specialty, you may not be aware of how the skill requirements have changed or how they may differ from one organization to another. If you have a reasonable level of skill in a high-growth area and are willing to learn, odds are you can pass most interviews for a high-growth job. If you're inflexible and unwilling to learn, you're in for a lot of frustration.

YEAH-BUT: There are no large companies in my town.

COACH'S COMEBACK: Most of the jobs being created these days are in small or startup companies. Find one near you that is growing, and get in on the ground floor, or join another small business that will provide services for it.

The U.S. Department of Labor has made projections of job growth in various occupations for 2002–2012. As you can see in the table on the next page, nursing jobs will grow by 27 percent while supervisory jobs in retail sales increase by only 9 percent. The message is clear: there are more opportunities for you in occupations that are growing.

TREND NO. 3: EMERGING DIVERSITY

One trend that touches every job candidate is the continuing diversification of the workforce.[1] This is good news for both employers and job seekers.

Non-Hispanic whites will continue to be the largest single group in the workforce; however, their numbers will fall from 71.3 percent in 2002 to 65.5 percent in 2012. By 2012 blacks, or African Americans, will increase from 11.4 to 12.2 percent, but Hispanics, or Latinos, will constitute a larger proportion of the labor force. Asians will continue to be the fastest growing of the four groups. The percentage of female workers will increase slightly.

The aging of the Baby Boom generation will cause the biggest shifts. Workers 55 and older are expected to increase from 14.3 percent to 19.1 percent by 2012, while the primary working age group, 25 to 54, declines from 70.2 percent to 65.9 percent.

Diversity encompasses more than just racial or ethnic segments of the population. The emphasis on individual and organizational values in the 1990s

FASTEST-GROWING OCCUPATIONS

Occupations with the largest projected job growth, 2002–2012 (*2004–05 Occupational Outlook Handbook*)

Occupation	Employment increase, 2002–2012	
	Number	**%**
Registered nurses	623,000	27
Postsecondary teachers	603,000	38
Retail salespersons	596,000	15
Customer service representatives	460,000	24
Combined food preparation and serving workers	454,000	23
Cashiers, except gaming	454,000	13
Janitors and cleaners, except housekeeping	414,000	18
General and operations managers	376,000	18
Waiters and waitresses	367,000	18
Nursing aides, orderlies, and attendants	343,000	25
Truck drivers, heavy and tractor-trailer	337,000	19
Receptionists and information clerks	325,000	29
Security guards	317,000	32
Office clerks, general	310,000	10
Teacher assistants	294,000	23
Sales representatives, wholesale and manufacturing	279,000	19
Home health aides	279,000	48
Personal and home care aides	246,000	40
Truck drivers, light or delivery services	237,000	23
Landscaping and grounds keeping workers	237,000	22
Elementary teachers, except special education	223,000	15
Medical assistants	215,000	59
Maintenance and repair workers, general	207,000	16
Accountants and auditors	205,000	19
Computer systems analysts	184,000	39
Secondary school teachers	180,000	18
Computer software engineers, applications	179,000	46
Management analysts	176,000	30
Food preparation workers	172,000	20
Retail sales first-line supervisors/managers	163,000	9

U.S. Bureau of Labor Statistics, Office of Occupational Statistics and Employment Projections (www.bls.gov/emp)

has trended toward the expression of one's personal and private life. Religious beliefs, sexual preferences, and political agendas are now workplace issues that often require one to take positions on topics other than job performance. At one time it was the norm to avoid discussing personal issues; today, speaking out is standard practice. This suggests a new skill for future success: the ability to express yourself nonconfrontationally while doing productive work.

YEAH-BUT: I'm a Caucasian male. Diversity doesn't concern me.

COACH'S COMEBACK: Yes, it does. You can have a competitive advantage over the Caucasian males who are not sensitive to diversity issues. If you can focus your attention on job tasks and team efforts without commenting on the personal differences between people, then you can be a better fit than many. It's okay to be aware of differences, but don't mention them.

These trends may sound boring, but they have great significance for every job candidate. First, tolerating diversity has become an important job skill. If you can't work with people who are different from you, you will be hobbled in both your job search and your career. Second, emerging diversity means that you will work in an evolving organizational culture, with unique priorities and issues. In short, it's good career sense to adapt to, if not embrace, these changes.

TREND NO. 4: THE DEMAND FOR CONTINUOUS LEARNING

I remember a time when education was best understood as an event—graduation! The question was "How much education do you have?" An acceptable answer would be along the lines of "a B.A. in marketing." But today, accelerating changes in the workplace mean that past education is only a want, whereas continuing education is a need in career management. According to U.S. Secretary of Labor Elaine Chao, "It all adds up to this: competency in a single skill will no longer last a lifetime. Workers today must come to lifelong learning and to continually upgrading their skills."[2]

I'm not saying that past education doesn't matter—it matters greatly. It's hard to become a college professor without a Ph.D., but the top-of-the-mind issues for employers are "What can you do for me right now?" and "What else can you learn to do for me next year, when everything changes?"

Regardless of how much education you have today, get more. In a report on tomorrow's jobs, the Bureau of Labor Statistics reports that education is critical for getting a high-paying job.[3] Forty-nine of the fifty highest-paying occupations require a bachelor's degree or higher; a bachelor's or associate degree is the most significant qualification for ten of the twenty fastest-growing occupations.

On-the-job training is the most significant source of education for another eight of the fastest growing occupations.

Think of it this way: If you don't get a degree, get a certificate. If you don't get a certificate, learn on the job. If you don't have a job, learn the job you want to get. With a target this big, all you have to do is try.

Education also has a lot to do with where you are most likely to get a good job. At one time, it was thought that the best strategy was to just go where there was a lot of growth. It made sense: "If you want a job, go where the jobs are." But today's reasoning is that if you want to get a high-paying job, go where there are a large number of college graduates. The more college graduates there are in an area, the greater its prosperity. The size of a city does not make it grow wealthy, but the education of its workforce does—and the wealth spreads into jobs that don't require a lot of education.

The percentage of people with college degrees varies widely among cities and regions. The American Community Survey of the U.S. Census Bureau[4] showed Seattle having the highest percentage of college graduates in the workforce age twenty-five and older (48.8 percent); Newark, New Jersey, was lowest (7.7 percent). A quick review of the cities in between (table, opposite) will give you an idea of what your prospects are in different regions.

YEAH-BUT: What if I don't have the exact skills they need?

COACH'S COMEBACK: Chances are, neither does much of your competition. Present the skills you have as thoroughly and impressively as you can. The employers will choose the best combination they can find, and they may consider many factors they haven't specified. Communicate the benefits of your particular package of assets.

TREND NO. 5: STRUCTURED INTERVIEWS

Employers are becoming more structured and systematic in assessing what candidates have to offer, for several reasons:

- Organizational change puts a new emphasis on job design and work quality. More thought is given to how each task contributes to an organizational objective. Knowledge of what needs to be done makes it easier to predict whether you have what it takes to do the job well.

- A hiring process that is structured to measure job skills will improve the overall effectiveness of people hired. Structured interviews are more reliable and valid than "gut feel" interviews.

PERCENT OF PEOPLE 25 YEARS AND OVER
WHO HAVE COMPLETED A BACHELOR'S DEGREE

Rank	Place	Percent
1.	Seattle, WA	48.8
2.	Raleigh, NC	48.0
3.	San Francisco, CA	47.8
4.	Washington, DC	42.5
5.	Atlanta, GA	41.2
6.	Austin, TX	40.6
7.	Minneapolis, MN	40.5
7.	Charlotte, NC	40.5
9.	Lexington-Fayette, KY	39.7
10.	Boston, MA	38.1
11.	Colorado Springs, CO	36.9
12.	Portland, OR	36.8
13.	Albuquerque, NM	36.5
14.	Oakland, CA	35.2
15.	San Diego, CA	34.9
16.	St. Paul, MN	34.6
17.	San Jose, CA	34.4
18.	Denver, CO	33.8
19.	Anchorage, AK	31.5
20.	Honolulu CDP, HI	31.4
21.	Nashville-Davidson, TN	31.1
22.	Pittsburgh, PA	31.0
23.	Arlington, TX	30.4
24.	Virginia Beach, VA	30.3
25.	Cincinnati, OH	29.6
26.	Omaha, NE	29.3
26.	New York, NY	29.3
26.	Columbus, OH	29.3
29.	New Orleans, LA	29.2
30.	Tulsa, OK	28.6
31.	Oklahoma, OK	28.3
32.	Kansas, MO	28.2
32.	Dallas, TX	28.2
34.	Houston, TX	28.1
35.	Los Angeles, CA	28.0

Rank	Place	Percent
36.	Indianapolis, IN	27.7
37.	Chicago, IL	26.9
38.	Tampa, FL	25.4
39.	Long Beach, CA	24.8
40.	Wichita, KS	24.7
41.	Sacramento, CA	24.4
42.	Aurora, CO	23.9
43.	Tucson, AZ	23.7
44.	Phoenix, AZ	23.5
45.	Miami, FL	22.2
46.	Corpus Christi, TX	21.6
47.	Jacksonville, FL	21.4
47.	Memphis, TN	21.4
49.	Anaheim, CA	21.3
49.	Fort Worth, TX	21.3
51.	Mesa, AZ	21.1
52.	Louisville, KY	20.9
53.	San Antonio, TX	20.8
54.	Riverside, CA	19.6
55.	St. Louis, MO	19.4
56.	Fresno, CA	19.3
57.	Philadelphia, PA	19.0
58.	Bakersfield, CA	18.7
58.	Las Vegas, NV	18.7
60.	Milwaukee, WI	18.4
61.	Buffalo, NY	18.0
61.	El Paso, TX	18.0
63.	Stockton, CA	17.3
64.	Toledo, OH	17.1
65.	Baltimore, MD	16.6
66.	Cleveland, OH	11.8
67.	Detroit, MI	11.2
68.	Santa Ana, CA	9.0
69.	Newark, NJ	7.7

Source: U.S. Census Bureau
American Community Survey Office
Last revised: August 25, 2004

- An unstructured process with vague selection standards raises suspicions of discrimination and invites legal problems.

Structured interviews are lists of interview questions designed to help the employer measure your skills and predict your job performance (see resource A). The questions are typically organized under "competencies," which are often referred to as "dimensions," "job factors," or "skills." All these terms refer to descriptions of the knowledge, skills, abilities, and other characteristics needed to do a job well. For example, here is a competency statement:

Innovation: Able to generate new solutions to existing problems; suggest changes/new procedures which will improve performance; suspend critical judgment to remain open to new perspectives; offer new ideas/methods to deal with opportunities and problems.

Organizations treat competency statements as selection standards, then develop questions to measure the competency. Here is an example of a question on innovation:

Describe a time when you were able to generate a new solution to an existing problem.

The interviewer will often have twenty or more questions about several different skills that are important for doing a particular job. For example, your interview may have questions on innovation, leadership, teamwork, adaptability, integrity, and organization.

This has special significance for how you prepare for an interview. Get ready to help the interviewer by giving specific information on exactly what you do well. For example:

- "I know twenty-seven software packages well enough to instruct end users."

USE WORKPLACE TRENDS TO YOUR ADVANTAGE

Trend	Action
Changes in jobs	Scan for opportunities and adapt
Occupational growth	Learn new skills for growth jobs
Emerging diversity	Prepare to accept differences
Continuous learning	Continually upgrade your skills
Structured interviewing	Anticipate giving skill answers

- "I regularly worked fifty hours a week in my last job."

- "I can write a newsletter with no grammatical mistakes."

- "I'm good at developing new business by cold-calling."

You may discover as well that you set yourself apart from other candidates by simply describing how your specific skills will benefit the employer.

BEYOND JOB MARKET TRENDS

Each of the workplace trends suggests broad themes on what you can do to prepare for the interview. Beyond these general directions lies a more specific challenge: how can you use this knowledge to ace the interview? It depends on the kind of interview, as you'll see in the next chapter.

Thoughts:

Thoughts:

THE FOUR
INTERVIEWER
STYLES

3

An interview is a little like a baseball game: you're the batter, the interviewer is the pitcher. Each pitcher is different; each has a repertoire of pitches that he can deliver, depending on his inclinations and the game situation. You need to be able to hit whatever he throws at you—fast balls, sliders, change-ups, screwballs, even the occasional slow, easy pitch. When you're standing at the plate, bat in hand, you can't know for sure what the next pitch will be. You must be ready to hit all kinds of pitches from all kinds of pitchers. You need to anticipate, prepare, and practice to get to first base.

But in crucial ways an interview is easier. Unlike a baseball game, an interview is a contest that both you and the interviewer can win. You can respond in a way that uses each question to your best advantage, while still satisfying the needs of the interviewer. It's as though you could grab hold of an incoming pitch and bring it over the plate at exactly the right spot, hit it safely for a double—and make the pitcher like it. Once you can read the interviewer's style and anticipate what kinds of questions she will throw at you, you will know how to respond in a way that meets her needs. In the interview game, your real competition is all the other batters, not the pitcher.

This chapter, by exploring the most common styles used by interviewers, will help you anticipate what the interviewer will say and do. Your assessment of the interviewer's style will help you manage your self-presentation and phrase your answers accordingly. Keep in mind, however, that most interviewers are not pure examples of any one type; every interviewer uses a different combination of approaches. But there is a way you can prepare for the unknown, and it's not as hard as you may think.

THE DIMENSIONS OF INTERVIEW STYLE

The model of interview style on the page opposite shows how to understand most of the different types of interviews you will encounter. Each of the two scales represents one aspect of interview style. The horizontal scale shows what kinds of information the interviewer tries to get from you; it ranges from person oriented at the left end to job oriented on the right. The vertical scale, which shows how the interviewer gathers and manages information, ranges from intuitive to structured.

In a person-oriented interview, the interviewer tries to discover your personal characteristics—the impressions you generate, your personality traits, your personal values, your feelings. A job-oriented interviewer, on the other hand, wants to know about your work experience, your skills, and your work habits in order to determine how well you might perform the tasks needed to get the job done. The job-related strategy is the approach industrial psychologists and attorneys typically recommend because, to be valid, the interview must be job related.

The vertical scale shows how the interviewer asks questions. An intuitive interviewer has no particular plan or agenda but asks questions spontaneously, as they come to mind, based on the interviewer's experience and impressions of the candidate. This type of interviewer usually takes few notes. A typical structured interviewer, by contrast, asks every candidate the same standard set of questions for that job, asks follow-up probes that relate only to the questions and takes extensive notes in order to recall and later evaluate your answers.

The structured approach may feel regimented, even rigid, but it is intrinsically fairer because it requires the interviewer to be more objective. The intuitive interview feels more open and relaxed; the interviewer asks questions as they occur to him, based on his feelings, perceptions and intuitions about you and your skills. This approach may feel comfortable, but it allows for subjective

INTERVIEW STYLES

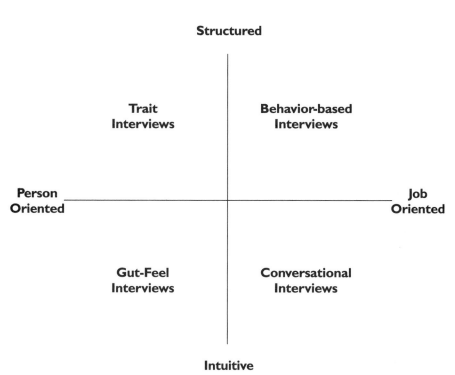

Structured

Trait Interviews

Behavior-based Interviews

Person Oriented

Job Oriented

Gut-Feel Interviews

Conversational Interviews

Intuitive

interpretation of your answers. It may also lead to problems if the interviewer carelessly asks a question about a legally protected topic.

There are four interview styles that come from our model:

- Gut-feel interviews are intuitive and person related.

- Trait interviews are structured and person related.

- Conversational interviews are intuitive and job related.

- Behavior-based interviews are structured and job related.

As soon as the interview begins, you will begin to pick up clues as to which of these four categories your interview falls into. Does the interviewer use a structured interview form? Are follow-up probes related to the job? Is she more interested in you as a person, or in your job experience and skills?

Regardless of which style the interviewer uses—and most use a combination of styles rather than a pure form—you will usually come out ahead if you respond by giving specific examples of things you have done that will provide evidence of your skills. This approach will satisfy the behavior-based interviewer; it will give the conversational interviewer the information needed to make a good decision; it will document your characteristics for a trait interviewer; and it will help you persuade the gut-feel interviewer that you will be a good fit for the job.

Instead of trying to analyze the interviewer's style during the interview, adopt a general strategy that will fit most styles. In answering most interview questions, give specific examples of times when you used a skill at work. This will enable you to prepare honest, accurate information about what you have to offer to the job. Then, if you can assess the interviewer's style quickly, you can modify this general strategy during the interview.

GUT-FEEL INTERVIEWS

The gut-feel interviewer uses a person-related, intuitive approach to see how you measure up to subjective selection criteria. In this type of interview, general impressions are used to select or reject you. There is no systematic attempt to gather information about your skills for doing the job. The gut-feel interviewer relies on intuition and subjective criteria to guide the interview and interpret answers. The problem for you is that it's hard—perhaps impossible—to figure

---

STEREOTYPES AND INTERVIEW QUESTIONS

Stereotype	Question
Overweight people are lazy.	"Are you willing to work through lunch most of the time?"
Playing contact sports builds competitiveness.	"What sports have you played?"
Women with children aren't career minded.	"How do you balance family with holding a full-time job?"
Religious people aren't much fun.	"How do you feel about going with us to happy hour on Friday afternoons?"
Sales people are money motivated.	"What type of sales contest do you like the best?"

out what these criteria are, or how the interviewer will assess whether you have the "right stuff." It's almost like a throw of the dice or a spin of the roulette wheel. But if this interviewer is between you and a job you really want, try to honestly emphasize the ways that you share this interviewer's experiences—this way, you have a shot at measuring up to what the interviewer wants to hear.

Many gut-feel interviewers think they can suitably assess the candidate's skills for the job within the first few minutes of the interview. This means that you will need to develop a positive first impression and keep it going during the entire interview. You cannot afford to relax your self-discipline and say the wrong thing, because this interviewer is prone to overreact to negative information. You can lose your positive momentum very quickly.

Gut-feel interviewers often base their decisions on their personal theories and stereotypes about success and failure. Many of these theories would seem hilarious to you—until you ran across one that denied you a job. A highly respected police commander once explained to me the most important factor in selecting police recruits: "Doc, I know it when I see it—he's tall." This theory of success, which was biased against women, failed to account for such critical factors as skills in coping, courage, adaptability, following procedures, and decision making.

SIGNS OF A GUT-FEEL INTERVIEW

- No structured interview form
- Questions based on personal theory of success
- Little or no reference to job requirements
- Emphasis on similar experiences
- Evaluation based on how much you are liked
- First impressions weigh heavily

Thoughts:

TRAIT INTERVIEWS

A trait interview uses an approach that is person related but structured. The goal is to measure key personality traits such as aggression, stability, and conscientiousness. In a pure trait interview, the interviewer reads questions off a structured interview form. But these questions relate more to personal characteristics than to job skills, often without reference to the kind of work to be done.

The pure trait interview has a solid foundation in both research and practice. It is often combined with personality tests administered by a psychologist or a highly trained personnel specialist. The interview and test information is then used to make inferences about the candidate's patterns of thinking or cognitive structures that in turn can be linked to the job. However, the trait approach can be poorly applied. The untrained interviewer can use individual traits to stereotype a candidate much the same way a gut-feel interviewer does.

QUESTIONS THAT TELL YOU IT'S A TRAIT-BASED INTERVIEW

"To what extent are you an organized person?"

"How do you evaluate yourself in terms of adaptability?"

"List your most positive qualities for me."

"Are you more aggressive or relaxed in problem solving?"

Preparing for a trait interview is straightforward. Identify the traits that correspond to the things you do well—for example, perseverance, leadership, organization. Have these words ready to use when describing yourself. Develop a short list of your negative traits that you can use to respond to negative probes, but try to state these negatives in as positive a light as possible. For example, one of your positive traits might be that you "like work that is challenging." Then be ready to admit to your negative trait: you are "too critical of people who do not put forth strong effort." Continue with a specific example of a time when you took on and accomplished a challenging task.

CONVERSATIONAL INTERVIEWS

The conversational interview is an unstructured interview with a casual exchange of job experience and job skills. It resembles a conversation between two equals. There's no prepared list of questions. Instead, questions seem to arise naturally out of the flow of the conversation, based on your responses and the interviewer's knowledge of the job. The conversation often branches naturally from one topic to another, as though the interviewer had no other purpose than to get to know you better.

This impression is misleading. The conversational interviewer uses rapport, rather than structure, as the principal tool for gathering information on your work skills. You may spend much of the interview in a friendly conversation about your general interests and personal experiences. Eventually, however, this interviewer will ask questions about your work experience, personal qualities, and values—things like integrity, work ethic, and open-mindedness. If you get into areas that are harder to discuss or that make you uncomfortable, he will steer the conversation back to areas where you feel more relaxed. By building and maintaining rapport, the conversational interviewer hopes to make you comfortable enough to reveal

YEAH-BUT: I want the interviewer to know about my experiences, personal qualities, and values. They will work to my benefit.

COACH'S COMEBACK: Good! The best way to communicate these things is to show how they have guided your behavior. For example, ensure that your values are not seen as being hot air. Describe what your values caused you to do in a specific situation.

important details about your qualifications and character that you might otherwise be reluctant to disclose.

If the interview is going well, you may feel as though you're just having a friendly chat about your work and career. This is a big mistake. You're being scrutinized the whole time—in the interview, at the coffee station, in the car, at lunch. You may feel comfortable, but remember: this interviewer uses the friendly approach to get as much information as possible.

Thoughts:

BEHAVIOR-BASED INTERVIEWS

A behavior-based interview is structured, but the questions are very different from the other styles. You are asked open-ended questions about past events that will provide information on your working habits and technical proficiencies. I believe this is the most reliable, valid, and unbiased method available for filling jobs with the best people, as far from a slapdash, gut-feel interview as you can get. It is often designed to be part of a selection system in which everyone uses the same technique—interviewers, the group manager, the human resources representative, the campus interviewers, and senior management.

QUESTIONS THAT TELL YOU IT'S A BEHAVIOR-BASED INTERVIEW

"Tell me about a situation in which you managed conflict successfully."

"Can you describe a time when you effectively told your boss some bad news?"

"Give me an example showing how you were supportive in a team."

"Describe a mistake you made at work that tested your coping skills."

"When did you use common sense to justify breaking a policy?"

Behavior-based interviewing is designed to acquire information about a person's past actions that can be used to predict how well she will perform on the job. This idea uses common sense and is academically supportable. Once we become adults, we tend to resist change. We develop habits, both good and bad, that are hard to break without concentrated effort. We also lose some awareness of these habits, so that when asked to describe how we behaved in a past situation, we tend to give a reasonably accurate picture of what we did. We may not even be aware that certain of these actions do not reflect well on us.

The behavior-based interview will be our point of reference through most of this book. My experience with effective and ineffective interviewers has taught me an important fact: The best way for a job candidate to approach most interviews is to use the principles of the behavior-based approach. When a marginal interviewer asks weak questions, respond as though you were answering a well-constructed question in a behavior-based interview.

OTHER STYLES OF INTERVIEWS

There are two other types of interviews that use behavioral principles: the simulation interview and the situational interview. These can be distinguished from behavior-based interviews by the time frame in the questions. Behavior-based interviews deal with past behavior; simulation interviews assess behavior in the present; situational interviews deal with future behavior. All are structured, and all deal with job skills.[1]

The Simulation Interview

In the simulation interview, you are asked to demonstrate specific skills by performing tasks. For example, the interviewer may say,

"Here's a paper clip. Sell it to me."

As you try to sell the paper clip, the interviewer may play the part of an unwilling customer, expressing doubts and objections, forcing you to deal with her sales resistance. Later, in her assessment, she may note how many benefit statements you made, how well you dealt with objections, and how skillfully you closed.

Preparing for the simulation interview is as basic as training yourself to do the job. This type of interview has the benefit of being directly related to important job tasks; you qualify for the job by showing that you can perform the tasks.

The Situational Interview

The situational interviewer asks you hypothetical questions, each presenting a dilemma for you to solve. For example: "You're the manager of a shipping dock in Chicago. It's the end of a difficult quarter. The shipping manager in Atlanta calls with an emergency. He asks you to help out by lending him a driver and a truck. If you do, you'll probably fall short of your goal and miss out on your quarterly bonus—but you'll be working as a team player, which is what your boss is always saying you should do. What would you do in this situation?"

Each of your answers is rated on its own scale; your total score is used to assess your overall performance in the interview. A good way to prepare for situational questions is to think through the difficult situations you have experienced,

EXAMPLES OF SITUATIONAL INTERVIEW QUESTIONS

"Assume that you are working in a warehouse that contains valuable computer equipment. You work alongside a good friend who helped you get your job. What would you do if you saw your friend stealing company property?"

"Imagine that you are running a cutting machine that is a critical part of the production process. It is the only machine that can do what needs to be done to meet an extremely important customer order. The machine is set up with an alarm system that will warn the operator when a dangerous malfunction is likely. However, in the last week the machine has been giving false alarms. What would you do if the warning siren went off on your machine?"

CHECK OUT THE INTERVIEWER

Put a check mark next to the phrases that best describe the interviewer's style in your last interview. Then ask yourself, how you could have best prepared yourself for that interview?

Gut Feel

___ Made little reference to job requirements

___ Made a quick decision about you

___ Asked favorite questions from memory

___ Seemed to be intuitive or subjective

___ Cut the interview short

Trait

___ Asked more about personal qualities than skills

___ Probed into your values and character

___ Seemed interested in how you think

___ Explored your values and feelings

___ Referred to a list of questions

Conversational

___ Built a trusting relationship

___ Moved easily from topic to topic

___ Asked general questions about career

___ Informally discussed the job culture

___ Showed concern for you as a person

Behavior Based

___ Took detailed notes

___ Asked about past work events

___ Seemed to be objective or fact oriented

___ Asked questions that linked to the job

___ Followed a written interview plan

identify what you've learned from them, and use this information to anticipate how you would answer questions. You should also make it a point to thoroughly understand the job and the organization. This will give you the strongest clues on how to present your answers.

LOOKING AHEAD

Now that you know more about the job market and what you can expect in the interview, you're ready to start the self-assessment that will prepare you to ace the interview. In the next part, you'll prepare yourself emotionally for the task of selling yourself. You'll learn how to profile your skills and competencies, to connect your skills with benefits for the potential employer, and to give specific examples of times when you used your skills. Not least, you will learn ways to anticipate and overcome those dreaded "killer" questions that you'd rather not have to answer.

Remember, you're not alone. Many people are looking for jobs today, even those who used to think theirs were safe. Having read this far, you're already better prepared to meet the challenge. You're pulled a little ahead of the field. The rest of this book will give you a true competitive advantage.

YEAH-BUT: It takes a lot of work to develop honest, specific examples that relate to my skills. Besides, I may need to fudge a little, because I don't have all the skills that the interviewer would like me to have.

COACH'S COMEBACK: You may be able to fool an interviewer well enough to get a job, but you won't be able to fool your boss well enough to keep it. In part two of this book, you will learn how to assess your skills. By giving detailed attention to developing specific examples of times when you used your skills, you will discover that you have more skills than you realized. That way you can be both well prepared and honest.

Thoughts:

Thoughts:

TAKE STOCK
OF YOURSELF

As one engineer put it, "It's cold, dark, and lonely out there. I used to think of a job search as a way to better myself. Now it's a matter of career survival. If my skills are not an exact match for the job I want, chances are someone else out there will get it.

"I'm shocked at how fast things are changing. The competition for good jobs is everywhere, and the candidates are strong and highly motivated. Plus, employers are insecure. It's like they're afraid of another economic downturn so they postpone job creation. I'm afraid that if things keep going like this I might stop trying. I'd work toward my fantasy career—start that ostrich ranch I've been dreaming about for years."

The engineer feels alone and fearful, disappointed with results, ready to bail out and become a rancher. That's the way many people feel, fighting the employment wars—so although he feels lonely, he's not alone. He has a tough battle ahead with his emotions, mainly to keep his lack of confidence from becoming self-perpetuating. He's scared that he "might stop trying."

This brief story touches on everything I'm going to tell you in the next group of chapters. Chapter 4 will tell you ways to recognize and harness the riot of emotions that you are probably experiencing and convert them to positive energy. Chapter 5 will help you profile your skills and understand exactly what you have to offer. Then, chapter 6 will show you how to convert your skills to benefits for the employer, and chapter 7 will explain how to share specific examples of times when you used your skills. Finally, chapter 8 will help you prepare dynamite answers to killer questions.

Altogether, this section is about getting ready through meaningful practice. Understanding is not enough—practical learning requires you to apply what you learn by practicing what to say and how to say it. This will prove to be the basis for your competitive advantage in the job market.

4

GET YOUR
HEAD ON
STRAIGHT

We all know someone who's an emotional disaster—some-one who overreacts to criticism, worries about things that can't be controlled, and fears rejection. Watching this person deal with a problem is watching a wreck about to happen. You want to say, "Get a grip on yourself! Chill out! Relax! Things will be okay!" But you know it won't do any good, so you don't.

And we all know someone at the other end of the scale—cold, detached, and aloof. This person doesn't seem to care about life or people. Emotionally oblivious to real problems, he doesn't react to things that are disasters for others; he lets things take care of themselves. He seems so removed, so dis-tant, that you want to say, "Hello, anybody home?" But, of course, you don't.

Who are these people? They are us—you and me—at times. You're probably like neither of these extremes—most of the time, at least—but sometimes you're fearful, nervous, excitable, and sometimes you're just too bummed out to get worked up about anything.

In the interview, some emotional states can help you and some can hurt you—and they aren't necessarily the ones you might think. The "negative" emotions of pain and fear often get in the way of action and confidence, but they can work to your advantage if you transform their energy into a determination to succeed in spite of your doubts. And the "positive" emotions of joy and confidence, although an important source of great energy and creativity, can work against you if you let them make you seem to be self-centered or arrogant. The challenge is to recognize how you feel without going to extremes. Stay in control, but show that you are career motivated.

It takes a level head to master your feelings without going to the other extreme and seeming aloof. Many people come across as detached or indifferent when things are tense—especially in an interview. This is the time when you have to tell yourself to get involved and show that you care. In the interview, level off your feelings; stay in control, but be warm and real.

LET THE FEELINGS FLOW

As you prepare for your interview, you will naturally experience a wide range of emotions, from "I'm in!" to "Aw, what's the use?" You'll sweat about your college transcript, grind your teeth over your last employer, turn cartwheels because you figure you've got the next job sewed up, and then go cold thinking about the unemployment line. Two hours later you'll be entertaining fantasies about sailing to Tahiti and living in a grass shack, painting masterpieces, and living on fish and pineapple with your soul mate.

These ups and downs are a normal response to the stress of anticipating the interview. They're like stage fright, an emotion that is rarely fatal but often helpful in getting ready for a performance. By the time you've finished preparing for the interview, your nerves will be steadier and you'll be composed and professional, even if the butterflies are raging just beneath your veneer.

Your best strategy is to let your emotions ebb and flow while you're preparing for the interview—that is, when you're alone and there's nobody around to be injured by the shrapnel. But keep your emotions under control when you're face-to-face with the interviewer.

YEAH-BUT: I've always been told just to be myself. Are you telling me to hide my feelings?

COACH'S COMEBACK: No. I'm telling you to control the expression of your emotions. This does not mean being dishonest—just practical. The way you feel, good or bad, about your job search can distract the interviewer from fully exploring your job skills. By controlling the feelings you express, you help focus the interviewer's attention on what you can actually do on the job.

This does not mean that you should act like a robot. If you're stiff and unresponsive, you'll seem cold and distant. That's not good. But if you're relaxed, if you've dealt with your feelings beforehand, you can respond respectfully and realistically, showing the right feelings at the right time.

Profit from Negative Feelings

Nobody likes to feel fear or anxiety. We put a lot of effort and attention into avoiding these feelings in everyday life. Yet they are inevitable, especially when we're put into new, unfamiliar, or dangerous situations. Major life changes are accompanied by just such uncertainties, and a job search is surely a sign of a major life change.

Pain and Frustration

A job search can involve a lot of pain and frustration. I've heard stories ranging from wounded dignity to financial ruin and broken families. But one of the most distressing things I have seen is the low-level, long-lasting pain that seems to hang like a little black cloud above people who have lost hope of finding good work. Whoever you are, whatever your skills, wherever you live, it can happen to you.

What can turn a skilled, motivated employee into a downtrodden chronic job seeker? A multitude of things, both personal and impersonal. The impersonal

---

AN EMOTIONAL AUDIT

Each of the emotions is presented in terms of opposites. Check the left-side or right-side emotion that is most characteristic of how you feel about your interviews. Then circle the emotions that you want to manage during your interviews.

Negative Emotions	**Positive Emotions**
___ Anxiety	___ Serenity
___ Anger	___ Joy
___ Withdrawal	___ Commitment
___ Worry	___ Confidence
___ Fear	___ Realism
___ Disappointment	___ Acceptance

include business trends that move the job market: downsizing, competition, technological change, world markets. Personal slings and arrows include every form of legal and illegal discrimination imaginable, promises made but not kept by people you trusted, and the humiliation of being laid off, with its implication that you are not as good as the others.

Often the frustration gets worse when common-sense solutions don't seem to work. You spend hours checking job postings on the Internet and get only one interview. Your day-to-day search gets stale and repetitive. Advice from your spouse, parents, or friends, however well-meaning, becomes trite after a few months. Your telephone becomes a recurring fixture in your nightmares. You'd love to hear about a job, but you hate to call new people to ask for an interview.

But if you can turn it around, you can make your pain work for you. When you channel it into a strategy, it can give you strength and conviction. Some derive strength from sharing experiences with a supportive friend or group. Others benefit from career counseling or from reading inspirational material. Still others treat pain as a challenge; they ask themselves hard questions, then answer them. Whatever works, do it. The energy you create by channeling your pain becomes positive energy for your interviews.

Fear and Anxiety

Fear is a feeling of apprehension about something specific. You may fear falling on the slippery floor outside the interviewer's office, or that a highly-qualified co-worker will get your promotion. The source of your fear is something that is very real, such as knowing that your interviewer actively discriminates against people like you. You can identify what you fear, and other people can agree that your fear has a reasonable basis in reality.

Fear can be a productive emotion. A reasonable fear of hazards keeps you alive and healthy. Even in the absence of physical danger, it can focus your

---

COACH'S TIP: Here are the positive effects of channeling pain into productive energy. Put a check mark next to the points you agree with.

____ Intense feelings can help you construct a vision of your dream job.

____ Psychological pain can motivate you to look for interview leads.

____ Negative emotions can lead to healthy exercise.

____ Bad feelings expand awareness of what you need to fix in your career.

attention on preparing well for an interview. It can motivate you to find out more about the skills needed for the job, to formulate answers to difficult questions you may be asked, to plan what you will say to avoid sounding stupid.

Anxiety is different, and harder to deal with. It is a diffuse fear—a generalized worry or apprehension about nothing in particular, or about something you can't quite put your finger on. Anxiety can range from a vague uneasiness to an intense and debilitating dread.

If you have interview anxiety, you have all the symptoms of fear without any obvious cause. You may feel anxious around authority figures because you had a bad sergeant in the army. You may be anxious about completing a written aptitude test because you once blew a college exam. But anxiety can also make you more alert to what can go wrong. It can help you anticipate difficulties and mobilize your efforts to deal with them.

KEEP A REIN ON POSITIVE FEELINGS

In normal, everyday life, we perform best when we balance our positive and negative emotions. We let good feelings steer us into new opportunities and enterprises, and we let our fear and the memory of pain stop us from blundering into great danger.

But sometimes positive feelings can limit performance—they can skyrocket, feed on themselves, and make us lose touch with reality.

Joy

It may seem strange to think of joy as something to avoid. But in an interview, joy is often linked to a relief from leaving a bad situation. This can be dangerous. Excessive joy can tip off the interviewer to any of several facts about you that don't necessarily help your case.

Perhaps you feel joy because you felt like a slave in your old job. That's understandable. But why did you stay there so long? Are you indecisive? Are your skills not good enough to get another job readily? Do you have an abnormal need for security, prestige, money? Was it a dictatorial boss, a poor working environment, or boring work that made you miserable?

Job stress and alienation can fuel unrealistic dreams of a second career and divert energy from your job search. You may feel relieved to be out of a disappointing career and have a general idea of what you want to do. The downside is that the intoxicating joy of relief becomes the status quo; energy is not channeled into effective interview preparation. You may feel great but say exactly the wrong thing.

I remember interviewing one candidate who was so relaxed that he seemed not to care whether he got the job or not. At one point he said, "I've got $50,000 in the bank and no debts. I've never felt so free in my life. I should buy my Harley and ride into the sunset!"

I thought to myself, This guy has no idea of how fast he can go broke. His $50,000 would have lasted him one year at best. After that, he'd never find a job paying what he could earn today. He was so happy to be "rich and free" that he failed to realize the value of advancing his career.

Channel your joy into a practical strategy, a design for your future. Then it becomes a productive joy, the joy of anticipation and practical optimism, based on your vision of a job that helps you become who you want to be.

Confidence

Confidence makes you more sure-footed, more eloquent, more polished—less likely to embarrass yourself in an interview. But confidence can work against you, too.

I know an expert on human resources management who is very capable and experienced in selection, compensation, job analysis, organization development, and training. Her credentials, and her confidence in her abilities, are so strong that, paradoxically, they have kept her from getting jobs that matched her skills. Less qualified interviewers saw her confidence and skill as a threat to their own career aspirations, not as a resource for the company, and would take pains to keep her from being discovered by other decision makers.

Your confidence can especially work against you if the interviewer perceives it as arrogance. Before you decide this point doesn't apply to you, remember that you are not the best judge of how the interviewer sees you. I have never heard a job candidate recognize arrogance as a reason a job was not offered. Arrogant people do not think of themselves as arrogant; they see themselves as decisive leaders with proven track records. If you think of yourself as confident, you should assume that some interviewers will think of you as having an exaggerated self-concept. Try to eliminate that perception before it happens.

You can reduce your chances of sounding arrogant by carefully managing how you use the word "I." This is not easy to do. Many interviewers will want to know exactly what you did in a particular situation, so you cannot altogether avoid the first person singular. But you can develop alternate speech patterns to describe your actions. Instead of saying, "This is what I did. . . . ," use a phrase such as "My contribution was. . . ." Rather than "I told them to. . . . ," say, "The suggestion was. . . ." This way you can minimize ego and maximize communication.

HARNESS YOUR EMOTIONAL ENERGY

You can use your emotional energy, positive or negative, to your own advantage by redirecting it, or channeling it, in positive ways. Been let down too often? Turn that disappointment around and transform it into determination not to let it happen again. Anxiety? Let it drive you to prepare yourself for the interview; you'll gain an amazing amount of confidence if you know the answers in advance. Anger? Don't get mad at the people who put you out of work, get mad at that unemployment line. Resolve to stay out of it. Joy? Sure, you're ecstatic about dumping that old job, but don't get giddy, get focused.

The first place to focus emotional energy is on honest self-assessment and interview preparation. The next four chapters will show you practical ways to identify and catalog your skills, match them with benefits for your potential employer, describe them persuasively, and deal with tough questions.

Thoughts:

Thoughts:

5

BUILD YOUR COMPETENCY PROFILE

As an industrial psychologist, I conducted thousands of individual assessments over a twenty-year period. These weren't clinical assessments dealing with emotional conflicts or adjustment problems—they were employment assessments, for selection, development, coaching, career planning, and job search.

Some of these one-on-one sessions were stressful, some were bland, but many others were interesting and enjoyable for both of us. Often the client would volunteer that it was a valuable experience, one that provided a new understanding of how to grow professionally. Always, though, the result was more than simple profiling. It was a snapshot revealing certain aspects of the person—competencies, weaknesses, issues, and feelings. The picture often revealed blind spots that could be approached only with great caution.

As a psychologist, I always felt privileged to be allowed to explore the hidden regions of the human psyche. I was often touched by what I learned—especially by those who were absolutely honest about themselves. By not holding back on the truth, they peeled away the façade of work life and let me gaze upon the real person within. They didn't always get the job, or the high score, or the praise for being clever. But they did get my respect, and a place in my heart forever.

Now you are going through an assessment process with me. But this is not a psychological profile; it's a competency profile, and it's designed to evaluate your work skills. We aren't face-to-face, but I want you to know that I can visualize you being honest with yourself. Together, we are going to do our best to describe what you can actually do for an employer. This will be the foundation for helping the interviewer see you as a person worthy of being hired.

UNDERSTANDING SKILLS AND COMPETENCIES

The competency profile we develop will be directed at *what you can do*, not *what you are like* as a person. Now, I know there's a part of you that is complaining, "I am unique!" or "My values are in the right place," or "I generate a great first impression." All these things may be true. But a trained interviewer wants information about what you can get done when you come to work. A good interviewer will show more interest in your work habits than in what you are like overall.

It's not easy to think about yourself objectively. You have a self-concept that has emerged over the years and that typically gets more solid, more fixed, over time. This helps you feel at home in your skin. Others can see you more objectively—but it can be painful to look at yourself through another's eyes. We like to avoid pain and move toward

> **COACH'S TIP:** Traits are words that describe the internal you. They show your patterns of thought, feelings, and motivations. Behaviors, on the other hand, are the external you; they are what you actually say and do. Employers are typically less concerned with your internal qualities and more interested in your actions. This makes it best to direct your self-assessment toward your skills and behavioral competencies. Therefore, your self-profile will describe what you can do and minimize who you are.

comfort, but personal growth is usually associated with discomfort. This time, it will be easier. We'll make a deal with each other—we'll look only at your career skills.

Skills are specific behaviors that can be seen or heard. You can see a physical behavior, such as a hand gesture, a smile, or a nod. You hear a spoken behavior, such as someone saying, "I am a good worker." In either case, a skill is observable when it can be demonstrated, verified by another person, and measured with a ranking or rating.

A competency[1] is a group of related skills that summarizes what you can do. Using competencies lets you understand, in general terms, the skill sets that you can bring to a job. It also lets you determine specifically which skills you have and which ones you need to learn—your "developmental areas"—in order to claim a particular competency. Thinking in terms of competencies helps you ensure that your self-assessment is reliably based on the specific things you have to offer.

Self-evaluation based on skills and competencies also enables you to focus on what you can do that is of value to an employer. It helps you avoid being distracted by discouraging information, bad feelings, unrealistic expectations, and other irrelevancies. Knowing exactly what qualifications you have for the job in terms of skills and competencies minimizes your anxiety and gives you confidence.

The skills-based approach also

COACH'S TIP: Be as objective as possible when describing your skills. Balance your choices to develop a representative picture of your positives and of skill areas that you need to develop. One way to do this is to assess alternately your strengths and weaknesses. First, give a high rating to your top skill. Then think in the other direction and give a low rating to your bottom skill. Continue changing your perspective this way until you have rated all of your skills.

gives you a window into the interviewer's mind. Many of today's more progressive organizations build a competency model based on the skills that are needed to fulfill their tasks and values. Then, they develop their interview questions based on their competency model. When you understand your own competencies, you can relate your interview answers to things an organization will want you to do.

Your self-assessment will enable you to describe the actions you take when doing work. It will not deal with your wishes, motivations, or innermost thoughts. It will help you get a realistic understanding of what you need to communicate to the interviewer.

TYPES OF SKILLS & COMPETENCIES

Your self-assessment will be directed to two general areas of measurement: competencies and technical proficiencies.

Competencies are groupings of specific working habits and performance skills used to reach a work objective. They may be learned at home, at school, or at work during any time of life. They may be enhanced by education, but their foundations are often set in life experiences. The same competencies can be used in many types of work—for example, leadership, organization, and problem solving are competencies that are used in a variety of jobs.

Technical proficiencies are the knowledge and tool skills used to perform particular job tasks. Such skills are typically taught in colleges or vocational schools—and, in some cases, an organization's training programs. For example, you may need to know statistics in order to manage a quality program, or you may need to have skills with tools such as a computer, an arc welder, or a microscope.

A substantial amount of research and professional opinion suggests that competencies may be further organized into people and task categories. For example, teamwork is a working habit that would be categorized as a "people" competency, whereas organization is a working habit that would be a "task" competency.

COACH'S TIP: Ask yourself the following questions about your own competencies.

- What experiences have taught you important competencies?

- How are your successes at work linked to your competencies?

- Which of your mistakes at work link to your competencies?

- How do your work goals relate to improving your competencies?

Look at the competency model (opposite page). You will see that competencies in the first group involve job tasks. For example, "Continuous Learning" is linked with the skill of being willing and able to "connect with coaches who teach." It is followed by a series of other, related skills that are the elements of the overall competency.

The competency model gives you an idea of some of the skills and competencies that the interviewer may look for in your background. You can select the competencies most relevant to your target job and be ready to answer questions about them.

You can also identify the technical proficiencies that are important to your specific occupation. Later, I will ask you to profile your technical competencies. When you develop your technical proficiencies profile, select the skills most important for your work and get ready to respond to questions about them.

BUILD YOUR COMPETENCY PROFILE

I'm going to ask you now to do a self-assessment using the Comp-A-Lizer, which stands for competency analyzer. The Comp-A-Lizer will help you build a profile of your competencies and technical proficiencies. You will need from thirty minutes to an hour, depending on how thorough you want to be. In my opinion, this is time well spent, because it will set the stage for your interview preparation.

Keep in mind that your self-assessment is only an estimate. You may have a blind spot that leads you to overestimate your skills and competencies in

A COMPETENCY MODEL[2]

Task-Oriented Competencies

A. Continuous Learning: Willing and able to connect with people who teach; learn from new jobs or assignments; set aside time to learn; convert mistakes into new learning; attend classes or training; ask questions to learn new skills.

B. Problem Analysis and Solving: Willing and able to anticipate problems; use mistakes to improve approach; define the causes of a problem; generate alternative solutions; involve experts in problem solving; use logic or math to analyze problems.

C. Goal Setting: Willing and able to commit to specific or challenging goals; convert performance gaps into goals; write goals that describe outcomes; involve stakeholders in goal setting; turn complex goals to learning steps; measure goal progress by milestones.

D. Organization and Planning: Willing and able to identify needed resources; use a time management system; develop contingency plans; maintain a record-keeping system; manage multiple details; use a calendar to schedule work.

E. Drive for Results: Willing and able to commit long hours to work; feel responsible for results; show a "can do" approach; persist in the face of obstacles; put work over socializing; push to get results.

F. Policies, Processes, and Procedures: Willing and able to use schedules to guide work; follow policies even if inconvenient; stick to important procedures; distinguish policies from guidelines; use procedures to simplify work; question ineffective policies.

People-Oriented Competencies

G. Resilience: Willing and able to turn pressure into productive energy; persist after setbacks and obstacles; turn a negative into new learning; bounce back from criticism; avoid negative comments and outbursts; use healthy methods to reduce stress.

H. Leadership: Willing and able to be an example for others to follow; be directive or participative based on the situation; build credibility and respect; ask for suggestions or participation; recognize others' contributions; guide others in the right direction.

I. Assertion: Willing and able to express opinions without apology; disagree without getting angry; describe feelings by calm repetition; stand up for rights or opinions; say no when you disagree; challenge authority respectfully.

J. Relationship Management: Willing and able to develop warm relationships; take time to listen; show empathy and concern; ask questions to understand feelings; disagree with respect; adapt to another's needs.

K. Teamwork and Collaboration: Willing and able to adapt to team needs; put team over personal wants; build trust with the team; contribute to the team; participate in team meetings; support team decisions.

L. Conflict Management: Willing and able to use conflict to clarify feelings; distinguish abuse from hot discussion; get feelings in the open; push on issues if necessary; convert discomfort to positive energy; take action to bring issues to the surface.

things like innovation, problem solving, or decisiveness. Or you can underestimate how much technical proficiency you have in areas like operations management, accounting, or employment law. The instructions for your self-assessment will help you be realistic with your estimates, but to develop a reasonably accurate competency profile, you have to bring an objective attitude about your skills.

YEAH-BUT: I know I don't have all the right skills for today's workplace.

COACH'S COMEBACK: You do have the right skills for some jobs. If you can speak reasonably well, read, and write, you have the basic skills required for many jobs. However, you may be asking this question because you're afraid you can't learn other skills that you need. Let me help you make your fear work for you. Answer this question for yourself: "Why don't I use my skills assessment as a starting point for future learning?"

I have taken the Comp-A-Lizer several times myself to experience what you will feel when you build your competency profile. Like me, you will probably resist rating yourself lower on some of the skills. But also like me, you need to remember that the Comp-A-Lizer will push some of your ratings out of your comfort zone in order to display a full range of information. This will help you discern which of your skills are stronger than others. Also, this approach will show the level of your skills relative to each other—not relative to other people. We are dealing with what you have to offer, not what you have to offer in comparison with other job candidates.

You will first rate the extent to which you have different work skills. Begin by reading over the competency model to get a preliminary idea of how they relate to you. Then, start on page 67, where you will find specific instructions on how to proceed.

YEAH-BUT: This competency profiling is a lot of detailed paperwork that I hate to do.

COACH'S COMEBACK: I understand—but what I'm asking you to do is what I would step you through if I were your face-to-face coach. The process of rating the skills and plotting your competency profile helps you test your assumptions about yourself. This will give you a realistic foundation for interview preparation.

Once you have completed your skill ratings and plotted your competency profile, connect all the points with a solid line. Put a plus (+) next to skills that meet or are in excess of requirements of jobs you may want; put a minus (−) next to skills that need development. Look at the sample completed competency profile on the page opposite to see what your results will look like.

A SAMPLE COMPETENCY PROFILE

Range

Competency	6–11	12–14	15–17	18–20	21–23	24–30
A. Continuous Learning						
B. Problem Analysis & Solving						
C. Goal Setting						
D. Organization & Planning						
E. Drive for Results						
F. Policies & Procedures						
G. Resilience						
H. Leadership						
I. Assertion						
J. Relationship Management						
K. Teamwork & Collaboration						
L. Conflict Management						

NEEDS IMPROVEMENT

STRONG POINTS

RÉSUMÉ

Before you plunge into the Comp-A-Lizer, take a few minutes to assemble your career information, including your résumé, certifications, degrees, and training experiences. Then, in the space below, list the skills you have that may be of value to an employer. When you are finished, go to the next page and read the instructions for the Comp-A-Lizer.

1. _____

   _____

2. _____

   _____

3. _____

   _____

4. _____

   _____

5. _____

   _____

6. _____

   _____

7. _____

   _____

8. _____

   _____

9. _____

   _____

10. _____

    _____

COMP-A-LIZER

The Comp-A-Lizer is a behavioral assessment tool that will help you identify competencies you have that are used in a broad range of careers. The profile you develop will help you assess your skills and decide what you need to emphasize in interviews.

It is important that you follow the instructions in order to build a profile that will realistically describe your strengths and developmental areas.

1. Look over your résumé or career information to refresh your memory of the competencies you have acquired over your career. Page 66 may help you summarize the skills that may be important to an employer. Once you have reviewed your skills, continue with the next step of these instructions.

2. Familiarize yourself with the list of skills you will be rating. Notice that there are six columns of skills on the next two pages. In front of each skill is a blank space where you can write your rating.

3. Read the rating anchors on the next page. Each anchor will help you assign a number to your skill level. Rate your stronger skills at the 4 or 5 level, your less developed skills at 1 or 2.

4. You will rate the specific skills that go into making a competency. The result will be a profile that shows the relative strengths of your competencies. Remember— you are not comparing your competencies to other people's competencies.

5. It is essential that you limit the number of times you use each rating level. In each column, limit yourself to one rating at level 1, three ratings at level 2, four ratings at level 3, three ratings at level 4, and one rating at level 5.

The rating anchors are on the next page. Use the anchors to help yourself apply a consistent standard when you rate your skills.

Thoughts:

Skill Rating Anchors

Level 1: Minor Extent. This skill is undeveloped when compared with my other skills. This may be a negative quality for which I need discipline or coaching. (There should be one level 1 rating in each in each column.)

Level 2: Limited Extent. This skill needs development in comparison with my other skills. It can limit my effectiveness, and there would be value in developing it. (There should be three level 2 ratings in each column.)

Level 3: Some Extent. This skill is in the mid-range in comparison with my other skills. It is available when needed, but secondary to my primary career skills. (There should be four level 3 ratings in each column.)

Level 4: Strong Extent. This skill is well developed in comparison with my other skills. It is a stable factor in my work effectiveness and usually generates positive outcomes. (There should be three level 4 ratings in each column.)

Level 5: Very Strong Extent. This is one of my best-developed work skills and can be used frequently or for long periods. I could coach others on how to use this skill. (There should be one level 5 rating in each column.)

Begin on the next page with step 1 and continue through step 5.

COACH'S TIP: It's more effective to work through one column at a time as you complete the Comp-A-Lizer. Alternate using the high and low ratings in the following way.

- Read and re-read the skill rating anchors until they are clear in your mind.

- Review the list of skills in column 1 of the Comp-A-Lizer on the next page. Select the skill that best fits the level 1 anchor and put a "1" next to it. Note that you may use the "1" rating only once in column 1.

- Next, read over the anchor for the level 5 rating. Review the list of skills in column 1 again, find the skill that best fits the level 5 anchor, and put a "5" next to it. Note that you may use the "5" rating only once in column 1.

- Continue with this approach for the level 2, 4, and 3 ratings. You may use only three level 2 ratings, three level 4 ratings, and four level 3 ratings.

- When you have rated all of the skills in column 1, continue in the same way for columns 2 through 6.

Step 3. Use the row totals from the previous page to profile your competencies. Circle a dot in each row to indicate the range the row total falls in.

Competency	6–11	12–14	15–17	18–20	21–23	24–30
			Range			
A. Continuous Learning	•	•	•	•	•	•
B. Problem Analysis & Solving	•	•	•	•	•	•
C. Goal Setting	•	•	•	•	•	•
D. Organization & Planning	•	•	•	•	•	•
E. Drive for Results	•	•	•	•	•	•
F. Policies & Procedures	•	•	•	•	•	•
G. Resilience	•	•	•	•	•	•
H. Leadership	•	•	•	•	•	•
I. Assertion	•	•	•	•	•	•
J. Relationship Management	•	•	•	•	•	•
K. Teamwork & Collaboration	•	•	•	•	•	•
L. Conflict Management	•	•	•	•	•	•

Step 4. You can now develop your technical proficiencies profile to accompany your competency profile. Build a list of technical proficiencies for your target job, which can be found on the occupational research page of O*NET OnLine.[3] This Department of Labor website will show the job tasks as well as the knowledge, skills, and abilities required in your occupation. Use this information to build a list of technical proficiencies important for your career. Then rate them on the following profile by circling the appropriate bullet.

YOUR TECHNICAL PROFICIENCIES PROFILE

Developed to a . . .

	Minor extent	Limited extent	Some extent	Strong extent	Very strong extent
Knowledge					
1. _____	•	•	•	•	•
2. _____	•	•	•	•	•
3. _____	•	•	•	•	•
4. _____	•	•	•	•	•
5. _____	•	•	•	•	•
6. _____	•	•	•	•	•
Skills with Tools					
1. _____	•	•	•	•	•
2. _____	•	•	•	•	•
3. _____	•	•	•	•	•
4. _____	•	•	•	•	•
5. _____	•	•	•	•	•
6. _____	•	•	•	•	•

Step 5. Your final task is to summarize your skills with brief notes on the form below. This exercise will give you a clear idea of exactly what skills you have to "sell" to a potential employer. Don't forget that a skill is an action that can be seen or heard as it is being performed. It is learnable, transferable, and work related. Thus, you can describe a skill as something that you are "able to" do.

MY SKILL SUMMARY

My competency profile describes both my strong points and my developmental areas as I see them. When I look over the separate skills and work habits that go into making a competency, I find that there are points for me to emphasize and avoid in my interviews.

I believe that my strongest competencies or skills are:

1. _____   4. _____

2. _____   5. _____

3. _____   6. _____

I believe that my strongest technical proficiencies are:

1. _____   4. _____

2. _____   5. _____

3. _____   6. _____

The most important things for me to showcase in the interview are:

1. _____

2. _____

3. _____

4. _____

5. _____

6. _____

I need to be careful when talking about the following developmental areas:

1. _____

2. _____

3. _____

TAILOR YOUR RESPONSES

Your success as a candidate will be greatly influenced by how effectively and honestly you can spotlight the skills you have that relate to each interviewer's needs. But the real challenge is to help the interviewer understand your strengths. With practice, you will find it easier to respond quickly to the interviewer's needs and express yourself convincingly.

In a typical interview, you won't know the interviewer's style until the interview has started. Therefore, you should go in with a thorough understanding of your strengths and weaknesses and without any preconceived notions about the questions you will be asked—that is, ready to adapt quickly to the interviewer's style and requirements.

The Comp-A-Lizer was designed to give you a more accurate picture of what your strengths are and how to present them to different interviewers, as well as a better knowledge of your developmental areas, which will help you avoid making damaging revelations.

The next chapter will help you fine-tune your presentation. You will learn how to make skill-benefit statements to describe your skills in terms of what you can do for the employer. You will be shown how to practice making these statements aloud, as you will when you talk with the interviewer in person or on the telephone.

Thoughts:

6

PREPARE
SKILL-BENEFIT
STATEMENTS

When you go to an interview, remember that the interviewer is a buyer, representing an organization that needs someone who can provide a set of skills to accomplish its goals. You are the seller, and your immediate task in the interview is to let the buyer know what skills you have and how those skills can benefit the organization.

What are your skills? Are they knowledge, things you know how to do in theory but have never done? Are they experience, combining knowledge with action? Do you have skills you are not aware of? Do you have skills that you alone are aware of? Do you offer charm and personality, with little practical knowledge? These are philosophical questions that bear on your self-esteem, your effectiveness, your earnings, your popularity—and your value to an employer.

For the interview, however, you must set aside such concerns and address the question that is paramount in the interviewer's mind: What can you do for us? To answer this question, you should respond with a set of skill-benefit statements.

In chapter 5, you summarized your strengths and connected them with your past experiences. In this chapter you will practice putting each of your skills and its benefits for your potential employer into a two-part statement. And you will begin to rehearse for the interview by reciting these skill-benefit statements aloud.

HOW TO MAKE A SKILL-BENEFIT STATEMENT

The way you communicate your value to the interviewer is to convert your competency profile into a set of skill-benefit statements. Each statement consists of two parts: (1) a description of what you can do, and (2) a benefit that you are able to deliver—in sum, your value to the organization.

A skill-benefit statement begins with a phrase that describes your skill. For example, here is a phrase reflecting a technical proficiency:

> "I can instruct and coach on the use of laser calibration instruments."

Note that the phrase uses "can," a word that emphasizes actions that can be taken. This is stronger than saying, "I know how to instruct and coach on the use of laser calibration instruments." Although in general they mean much the same thing, "can" conveys that you not only know *how* but are also *able* to use the skill. "Know how to" says only that you understand what to do.

Then, to complete your skill-benefit statement, simply add an implication to the skill statement. This happens when you include "able to" in the statement.

COACH'S TIP: A skill-benefit statement encourages you to talk in a way that combines "I can" with "able to." For example: "I can write software that works with your system, so I am able to set up your reports for you to reorder supplies at exactly the right time."

CONVERT YOUR SKILLS TO BENEFITS

Take a skill from your competency profile and make a skill-benefit statement:

My skill is _____.

(Skill-benefit statement) I can _____,
                                              (skill)

so I will be able to _____.
                          (benefit to the employer)

"I can instruct and coach on the use of laser calibration instruments. So I am able to begin training your people on the day I start to work."

Notice that the benefit communicates how the skill is of value to the interviewer. "Can do," plus "able to," plus a benefit, is a powerful phrasing.

Note that the implication expresses the results you can deliver. It also assumes that a job offer will be made. It says, "on the day I start to work for you," not "if I start to work for you." The wording reflects confidence that a job offer will be forthcoming.

Avoid Ego Trips

There's a big difference between making skill-benefit statements and bragging. A braggart is quite capable of self-entertainment—perhaps even forgetting about the interviewer. If you find yourself rattling off all the wonderful things you have learned how to do in your life, you're probably bragging. You've lost sight of what the interviewer wants: Information needed to make a good hiring decision.

YEAH-BUT: I've always been told to avoid saying "I" too much, but most of your examples suggest using "I."

COACH'S COMEBACK: You're right. Using "I" too much may give the interviewer the impression that you have a big ego. However, for these exercises I have asked you to use the word "I" on purpose to help you identify exactly what you have to offer. Once you have done this, you can use your skill-benefit statements as part of your past work experience, which can include recognition of team efforts and the resources that others made available to you.

Pay close attention to what the interviewer asks you about a specific skill. Focus your answer on the value the organization can derive from your skill. A well-framed skill-benefit statement helps the interviewer make a good decision for the organization, for you, and for other candidates. You may be better off not mentioning some of the skills you are most proud of. They may seem important to you, but if they don't relate to the employer's needs, you're wasting the interviewer's time by talking about them. Some of the skills you value most highly may even seem frivolous to the interviewer; do many organizations need the services of a bass guitar player? A skilled weight watcher? An amateur archeologist? It's better to emphasize the skills the interviewer asks you about, regardless of the ones that you value the most.

Above all, don't use the interviewer as a captive audience for the story of how great you are. Describe your skills and how you can use them for the interviewer's organization, not what you are like as a person. After all is said and done, today's employer is more interested in how fast and how well you can use a skill than in hearing about your wonderful qualities.

HOW TO USE SKILL-BENEFIT STATEMENTS

Formulating skill-benefit statements is only one step in preparing for your interview. You must be natural as you present them. Don't just recite a canned list of your skills and their value to the employer.

I once knew a salesperson who would hammer potential customers with benefits. His presentation was fast, specific, and to the point. There was no doubt what he thought of his product. However, his approach probably lost more customers than he gained.

Think of how you carry on a conversation with a friend. Whatever the subject matter, you don't simply throw out random observations, or interrupt with remarks that have nothing to do with what your friend is talking about—at least, not if you expect to remain friends. You follow the flow of conversation, interjecting your own comments where appropriate.

A good interview should be as mutually satisfying as a good conversation. You should pay careful attention to what the interviewer is saying and, with appropriate timing, weave your skill-benefit statements into the conversation.

SAMPLE SKILL-BENEFIT STATEMENTS

"I can work with difficult people, so I will be able to fit in wherever you want me."

"I can develop an up-to-date policy manual that is consistent with EEO, ADA, OFPC, and OSHA regulations, so I'll be able to develop your manual in a timely and professional manner."

"I can provide sensitive patient care in an AIDS pediatric unit, so I am able to be an effective member of the team by next Monday."

"I can run the digital lathe on the night shift, so I am able to help you make production quotas during the busy season."

"I can develop a marketing plan, write ad copy around it, and develop a quality sales training program. So I am able to produce immediate results in the marketing department."

"I can make money. I am able to have billings that exceed my salary within one month."

"I can reengineer a work group by analyzing work processes and finding bottlenecks. I am able to improve performance in record time."

"I can type eighty words per minute. I can take shorthand. I can file with absolute accuracy. I am able to make your job easier for you."

SKILLS AND PROFICIENCIES BENEFIT STATEMENTS

Review your skill summary on page 73. Then list your top six competencies and technical skills on the page below. Insert the skill after the "I can" and continue with a benefit that follows "able to."

Skills

1. I can _____,
   so I will be able to _____.

2. I can _____,
   so I will be able to _____.

3. I can _____,
   so I will be able to _____.

4. I can _____,
   so I will be able to _____.

5. I can _____,
   so I will be able to _____.

6. I can _____,
   so I will be able to _____.

Technical Proficiencies

1. I can _____,
   so I will be able to _____.

2. I can _____,
   so I will be able to _____.

3. I can _____,
   so I will be able to _____.

4. I can _____,
   so I will be able to _____.

5. I can _____,
   so I will be able to _____.

6. I can _____,
   so I will be able to _____.

Just as in any friendly conversation, strive for honesty and modesty. Base your delivery and emphasis on the importance of the topic, as indicated by the interviewer's question. It is important for you to practice saying these skill-benefit statements aloud. It's a lot like rehearsing for a speech or a play; the sound of your voice becomes more familiar to you, and you cán picture yourself actually saying these things to the interviewer. You gain confidence.

There is, however, an important difference between practicing skill-benefit statements aloud and learning your lines in a play. In the interview, you don't know exactly what the interviewer is going to ask. You must be ready for anything. Therefore, it is the format that you're practicing, not the exact wording you'll use. You need to get comfortable with the process of framing your qualifications in the form of skill-benefit statements—not memorizing an unchanging script.

Adapt to the Interview

Just as your tone, emphasis, and attitude will naturally vary in the course of a lively conversation, you should use a variety of techniques to present your skill-benefit statements as you respond to the interviewer's questions.

Sprinkle benefits. Season the interview like a gourmet dish by offering a range of skills:

- You can develop biodegradable plastics, so you are able to have a positive impact on the environment, and . . .

- You can supervise large teams of researchers in product development, so you are able to meet ambitious research goals, and . . .

- You can write for both scientific publication and marketing, so you are able to help the advertising department write accurate promotional materials.

This approach is helpful in a panel interview; offering a variety of benefits raises your chances of mentioning at least one skill that will interest each interviewer. It is especially useful when you don't know very much about the job you will be doing. Sometimes even the interviewer doesn't know exactly what your job will be; using the sprinkle approach, you'll cover so many skills that some are sure to be appropriate for whatever the job turns out to be.

Target benefits. In order to prepare honest, accurate skill-benefit statements that match the job requirements, you need to know what tasks your target job entails. If this information is not available from the employer, you can look up the job tasks for the occupation in the Department of Labor's "O*NET OnLine."[1] Reviewing a prepared list of tasks for your job will enable you to select a representative group of tasks that you do well. Then, in the interview, you can emphasize a specific area of technical experience that other candidates may fail to mention. Target competencies also, by reviewing the information in the "Work Activities" section. Being specific about the benefits you offer can pay off big.

Compare and contrast. Whenever you can do so without sounding negative, communicate your skill level by comparing or contrasting your work with the good work of others. Show your breadth: "I can perform most of the stress-distribution analyses that Ph.D. engineers did on my last job." Describe an improvement that you made: "I used my knowledge of personnel systems to develop the first performance-based compensation program at Grace Hospital." It's best not to sound critical of your co-workers or your organization; remember, comparing your skills with a higher standard can only enhance them in the interviewer's eyes.

COULD DO VS. CAN DO

It is tempting to think that you *can* do something just because you understand *how* to do it. This is not necessarily true. You may understand how to make skill-benefit statements, but you should write them out and practice them aloud. Simply believing that you *could* say them, if you had to, doesn't mean that you *can* say them, especially under the pressure of an interview.

I asked several people to write skill-benefit statements and then comment on what they learned by doing so. Here are some of the things they said:

"At first I couldn't write down more than four benefits. So I had lunch with some of my co-workers, and they basically told me some skills I had that I didn't even know about."

"It was pretty easy for me to do. I completed thirty-three skill-benefit statements for the categories that were relevant to my career. Then I revised my résumé to reflect a greater breadth of skills."

"I got my mother to do it for herself. She has not worked outside her home for twenty-seven years. A lot of what she has done converted to skill statements."

"I was surprised to see a big gap between what my values are and my 'can do' statements. It seems that I don't act on my values as much as I thought I did."

Show and tell. Bring a work sample to the interview and describe the skills you used in developing it. A program developer I once interviewed for a job brought several examples of her work. As we looked at what she had done, she described the steps that she had taken in developing the programs. When I asked technical questions, she replied with skill-benefit statements; these and her work samples showed me that she was skilled in creating development software and aware of the problems faced by a corporate trainer.

Share credit. Even though you need to impress the interviewer, don't foster the impression that you see yourself as the single cause of your successes. Describe the opportunities you were given, then explain what you did to take advantage of them. Acknowledge the skills of the teams you worked with; allude to the synergy that resulted when you lent your skills to the team effort. Identify the important aspects of an organization's culture that helped mold and refine your skills for the good of all. Giving ample credit to the source, recognize what you were taught by a mentor or teacher and describe the skills that grew from the experience.

Watch your body language. During the twenty years that I conducted selection interviews, I was usually more conscious of what candidates were saying than of their nonverbal signals. However, I did take notes on the body language and gestures that accompanied some of their answers. When I reviewed five years of my interview notes, I was astonished to see how many times I wrote down such comments as "hands to face" and "leaning forward." I now realize that my impressions of candidates were influenced by these nonverbal messages—and that most interviewers are similarly influenced, consciously or unconsciously.

Moving one's hand to the face is a sign of discomfort or lack of confidence. Leaning forward and nodding affirmatively reflects pride and confidence. This suggests to me that when you make skill-benefit statements you should sit up and lean forward. Keep your hands away from your face; the table or your lap is a good place for them.

End with a benefit. A good conversation flows smoothly when one participant follows through on the last thing said by another. If you end your answer by stating a skill-benefit, you will increase the likelihood that the interviewer's next question will deal with your skill. This technique is especially good at steering the unstructured interviewer—the one without a list of prepared questions— to keep the interview focused on the skills to be assessed. But it will also help you deal with a structured interviewer by bringing to his attention additional topics that may help your case.

Each of these techniques is based on your ability to formulate a number of honest, accurate skill-benefit statements—a process you can begin by converting the skill profile you constructed in the last chapter to a series of brief statements that you can use as needed in your interviews.

PUTTING IT ALL TOGETHER

By completing this chapter, you have reached an important milestone in interview preparation. If you finished all the exercises, you now have several skill-benefit statements to use in selling your skills to the interviewer. This will make you a standout candidate. And—perhaps more important—you should have a better idea of what you have to offer. Having practiced stating aloud your skills and their associated benefits, you should have more confidence now that you can handle yourself in the interview. Your confidence will be self-evident; it will be real and honest, because it is based on your skills.

You now have the foundation you need to advance to a more thorough way of answering questions the interviewer asks you. In chapter 7, you'll learn how to invest your answers with more detail and experience by describing times when you actually used the skills that you've described in your skill-benefit statements. And you'll get more practice in describing your qualifications aloud.

Thoughts:

Thoughts:

7

GET SPECIFIC WITH SHARE ANSWERS

Storytelling is an ancient tradition, a way humans have of passing along experience and knowledge to others. In everyday conversations, we tell stories about ourselves—what situations we found ourselves in, who was there, what was said, how we felt, what we did, and so on. It is an effective and entertaining way of making contact with others, sharing our experiences, making sense of the world, justifying our actions.

In an interview, you are called upon to accomplish many of the same things. You are asked to talk about your knowledge, your skills with tools, your abilities, your work habits—all the things that qualify you for the job. Unlike a casual conversation, however, the interview is a place to be specific, rather than general—to tell honest stories about yourself that highlight specific skills.

To communicate that you have a skill important for doing the job, it is best to tell the interviewer what you did in a situation in which you used that skill. Your story needs to include all the relevant details about the situation, the hindrances, your actions, the results of your actions, and the outcome. And you need to share this information quickly, clearly, and accurately.

FORMULATING A **SHARE** ANSWER

Instead of talking about feelings and generalities in your answers, you need to give candid, accurate examples of times when you used specific skills. The SHARE technique is a guide for preparing these examples and showcasing your skills. A SHARE answer provides specific information on the situation, hindrances, actions, results, and evaluation of your example. Here's how it works:

Situation: Begin by describing the situation in which you were operating.

Hindrances: Explain any constraints or hindrances on what you did.

Actions: Describe exactly what you did.

Results: Cover the results that can be attributed to your actions.

Evaluation: Summarize the effectiveness of your actions.

Using the SHARE technique, prepare fifteen to twenty examples, as honestly and completely as you can, of times when you used different skills at work. This gives you time to survey your skills so you can be clear, accurate, and comfortable in the interview. Having several accurate answers on the tip of your tongue makes you better able to answer difficult questions. You will project your best image, rather than your nervous image.

Take special care to answer the question that was asked. This may seem so obvious as to be barely worth mentioning, but I've been astonished over the years at how often qualified, able candidates don't really answer the question that was asked. Sometimes, of course, this can mean simply that they have misunderstood or are so nervous that they begin answering without taking time to think. But it's important to avoid giving the impression that you aren't very good at listening or following instructions.

COACH'S TIP: When you take the time to develop specific answers, you're doing more than simply preparing for specific questions. One of the biggest benefits you will get is confidence. Knowing what to say will make you comfortable and smooth in the interview.

PRESENTING YOUR SHARE ANSWER

In my experience as an interviewer, candidates who give focused, specific, and relevant answers use some combination of these steps:

1. Listen carefully to the question, perhaps restating it to confirm your understanding.

2. Ask for clarification, if necessary.

3. Look to the side and pause to think of an example that will answer the question.

4. Answer the question candidly and specifically, using the SHARE model.

5. Ask whether your answer addresses the question.

Don't follow these steps mechanically, as if you were programming your cell phone; if you do, you'll end up sounding like a robot. Use common sense; be flexible.

Practice using the questions on page 91; become familiar with them; try out variations. Then, in the interview, let the interviewer's approach and the specific questions guide your answers.

Skilled interviewers will ask you ten to twenty questions in an hour. Each of your answers should use at least some components of the SHARE model. You may be tempted to ask the interviewer to reuse your answer to a previous question; resist the temptation. Each question you are asked gives you a new opportunity to communicate your fitness for the job; each answer you give helps your cause even more. Be prepared to give specific answers to many different interview questions, and use each example to demonstrate the skills that you have.

YEAH-BUT: Is it really worth my time to do all this preparation? If I'm too prepared, my answers will sound canned.

COACH'S COMEBACK: Wrong! Preparing specific interview answers will take you only two hours or so—time that will make you a stronger competitor in your interviews. And it's not preparation that makes you sound "canned," it's incomplete preparation. In order to be really good in your interview, practice giving specific examples of your skills aloud until you feel comfortable doing it.

AN OUTSTANDING SHARE ANSWER

There are few things better than a good story to lend energy to an interview, and a good yarn presented in the form of a SHARE answer has the added benefit of driving home a point about your skills. I once asked a retired paratrooper I was interviewing to give me an example of a time when he had to cope with a difficult situation. After a few moments of thought, he began to tell me about a survival program he had undergone as part of this military training:

> After parachuting into the training area, we had the mission of avoiding capture. If we were captured, our mission was to escape. As it turned out, we were 'captured' within hours by the 'enemy'—the training staff. Their 'prison camp guards' interrogated us and put us in their lockup.
>
> This was supposedly a secure area. It had a dirt floor and crates for us to sleep on. But I found a tunnel under my crate that apparently went under the fence and out of the compound.
>
> I quickly organized three of us into an escape team and we started to crawl down the tunnel. It opened into a space about three feet deep and wide and continued for about twenty feet, and then it came to a dead end. I told the other two guys to back out and we'd try again. But the hole had been covered up with something heavy. We were stuck.
>
> One of the guys panicked, screaming to be let out, but I got him to calm down by saying that we had obviously been set up, that the tunnel was a trap, but that it was only an exercise and we'd get out okay. I talked about what we would do later to celebrate surviving the school—we'd go to Hawaii. By the time I got around to describing our beach party, he had settled down. Within an hour or so we were released.
>
> Now, when I think back on what happened, I feel that it was a profound learning experience for me. I learned that being calm is an important part of problem solving. And I learned that I could exert leadership in helping another person cope with a difficult situation.

I was spellbound by his story. Not only did he answer exactly the question I had asked, he used the SHARE format very effectively to illustrate his skill in coping. He described succinctly the difficult situation he and the others had found themselves in; told of the hindrances that arose as they tried to solve problems; explained exactly how he used his skills to overcome those hindrances; told me the results of his action; and related effectively what he had learned from the experience. Besides conveying what an adventure it was, he showed that he could be a calming influence on others and that he was willing and able to be a leader.

Of course, a natural storyteller has an advantage over others. Perhaps you don't think of yourself as a skilled communicator, but as you practice putting together your SHARE answers, think of the most dramatic examples you can of each of the skills you want to highlight. Maybe you've overlooked a good example or two. Don't make up tall tales, though, or paint yourself as a super-hero for every situation, or try to make your work history sound like an endless series of adventures. One or two good examples mixed in with natural conversation will be sufficient to heighten the interviewer's interest.

PREPARING YOUR OWN SHARE EXAMPLES

You will now develop SHARE answers for communicating how you can use your working habits on the job. First, review the sample SHARE answer on the next page. Next, review the skills and questions that might be asked by a behavior-based interviewer. Then write out a SHARE example for each of the skills that you may want to showcase in the interview. Remember that your Comp-A-Lizer results (pages 71–73) can help you identify what you want to emphasize.

This is an especially valuable exercise for three reasons:

1. It gets you into the SHARE answer pattern.

2. It helps you identify and remember the many individual skills that you have developed in your career.

3. It makes you think through how you will answer similar questions in the interview.

Having in mind examples to discuss will build your confidence and impress the interviewer.

Once you have developed a respectable set of SHARE answers about your competencies, you have several important tasks in front of you. First, you need to develop SHARE answers for your technical proficiencies, those you identified in chapter 5. Each of these skills is described in general terms, because there are so many different technical proficiencies any reader could have. Choose the categories that apply to you, and develop SHARE examples to illustrate your technical proficiencies.

You may have noticed that, although most of the questions for which you composed SHARE answers in this chapter were positive questions, I included some negative queries to remind you that some interviewers will ask

SAMPLE SHARE ANSWER

Competency: Leadership—willing and able to be an example for others to follow, to be directive or participative based on the situation, to build credibility and respect, to ask for suggestions or participation, to recognize others' contributions, and to guide others in the right direction.

Skill: Able to be directive or participative based on the situation.

Question: "Give me an example of a time when you were a participative leader."

Answer (applying the SHARE technique):

> **Situation:** "During one project, I was assigned as leader of a team to put together a catalog that one of the other team members had done by himself in the past."
>
> **Hindrance:** "It quickly became apparent that this team member didn't like having his personal project taken away from him and assigned to the whole team. I know that he had strong feelings about it, not just because it was his idea originally but because he was concerned that the quality would suffer."
>
> **Action:** "I went to his office and started asking questions to get him to participate in building a solution to the problem. Along the way I asked him how he felt about helping the other team members maintain the quality standards he had set. I asked him to call a meeting at his convenience to describe the problems he had encountered in past issues and to tell us how he had overcome them. I explained that if the team did a good job, we would probably be assigned many more publications than any one person could handle, so future publications would probably be shepherded by individual team members with the help of all the other members."
>
> **Result:** "He immediately became enthusiastic about helping to increase the team's responsibilities. He volunteered not only to conduct a brief training session but to consult with each team member as problems arose. Before I left his office, he told me of several improvements he had been thinking about for the next issue and offered to share them with the team at the meeting."
>
> **Evaluation:** "I felt that by involving him in the solution to the problem I helped him see that the project had matured and grown too large for any one person to handle; that his experience would be more valuable spread among several publications; and that his good work in the past had put him in line for more responsibility."

you for negative examples as well. For example, the question under Resilience was "Tell me about a time when you were not able to bounce back from criticism." The question under Policies, Processes, and Procedures was worded as follows: "Give me an example of a time when you decided to break a policy and got bad results."

To be doubly prepared for a behavior-based interview, formulate SHARE examples to use for negative questions. But try to frame your answers in a positive light. Explain what you learned from the experience, or tell the interviewer how you were able to solve the problem by using other competencies or technical proficiencies.

COMPETENCIES AND SAMPLE QUESTIONS

Respond aloud to each question with a SHARE example.

Resilience: "Tell me about a time when you were not able to bounce back from criticism."

Assertion: "Give me an example of a time when you were able to express your opinions directly, even when there was going to be disagreement."

Drive for Results: "Describe a time when you were not willing to commit long hours to work."

Goal Setting: "Tell me about a specific time when you converted a performance gap at work into a specific, measurable, and realistic goal."

Organization and Planning: "Please share an example of a time when you developed a plan that was a systematic use of available resources."

Policies, Processes, and Procedures: "Give me an example of a time when you decided to break a policy and got bad results."

Teamwork and Collaboration: "Describe what you did in a teamwork situation that shows how you could adapt your interests to team needs."

Leadership: "Give me an example of a time when you were not successful in influencing others to take effective action to reach a goal."

Conflict Management: "Tell me about a time when you were able to use conflict to clarify feelings."

DON'T FORGET "WHAT IF" QUESTIONS

The popularity of behavior-based interviewing means that SHARE examples, which come from your actual experience, will work well for you most of the time. There is a possibility, however, that you will find yourself in a situational interview, in which you are asked hypothetical questions.

In a typical situational interview, several people read you ten to fifteen prepared questions about what you would do in specific situations.[1] (Look on page 45 in chapter 3 for a quick refresher on how situational questions are worded.) These questions pose dilemmas that require you to choose a course of action—a choice that reveals which of your work habits you are most likely to use on your next job. Answers are scored using rating information provided by job experts. This makes the situational interview systematic, objective, and a reliable measure of your skills.

Your SHARE examples can help you prepare for situational interviews. Being clear about what you *did* do will help you be clear about what you *would* do. You can also talk about your future actions in ways that take advantage of what you have learned from mistakes.

WHEN THE GOING GETS ROUGH

It's easy enough to answer straightforward questions about your skills if you're prepared and have practiced using the skill-benefit and SHARE formats aloud. But how do you respond when the questions get personal, pointed, embarrassing, invasive, hostile, or even illegal? As you will see in the next chapter, the SHARE technique can be adapted to fit almost any situation, even the tough ones. You will learn how to answer these "killer questions" calmly while doing as little damage as possible to your interview ratings.

Thoughts:

8

KILLER QUESTIONS, DYNAMITE ANSWERS

What's the thing you fear most about being interviewed? Being asked a question you can't answer or don't want to answer, right? Sooner or later, someone will ask you that killer question. Incompetent or mediocre interviewers will ask you questions that are illegal, irrelevant, incomprehensible, or intended simply to trip you up. A good interviewer will ask you questions that challenge you, stretch your ability to answer, and let you demonstrate what kinds of skills you have to offer.

Don't worry; for every killer question, there's a good, honest answer. As long as you're prepared to answer in a way that will keep you in the running as a candidate, you don't have to fear killer questions. Some of the questions can even be used to your advantage. If you can give a dynamite answer, you can earn extra points from the interviewer.

In this chapter you will learn how to use the techniques you've learned so far to respond to these questions. You can adapt your skill-benefit statements to make your point quickly or use the SHARE answer format when you need to document exactly what you did. Regardless of which approach you take, remember that your objective is to use every question, no matter how adverse, as an opportunity to demonstrate what you can do on the job.

IN THIS CORNER, THE KILLER . . .

There are several kinds of killer questions. The following list shows the range—from the offensive to the clever.

Illegitimate questions. Questions relating to a candidate's gender, race, color, national origin, religion, age, or disabilities are subject to legal scrutiny. Women probably get asked the most inappropriate questions—those about children. "How will you take care of your children when they are sick?" is out of line; it assumes that the mother will have problems with child care. Whether asked of women or men, probes into family, home, and personal life are questionable, but not uncommon.

Personal theory questions. Managers develop their own personal theories about success. Some are based on practical observation of how successful performers usually behave. Some interviewers, however, cannot get past certain irrational notions, such as the theory that graduates of a particular university (the interviewer's) are prone to success, or that athletes make the best salespersons. It's hard to overcome a personal theory—it's a silent obstacle. You don't know what it is or whether it will work for you or against you. The only thing you can assume it that it is there.

COACH'S TIP: In a fencing class, you quickly learn the importance of the phrase "en garde." It means to be ready for whatever may come your way. Many candidates miss out on good opportunities by mishandling a single question. You have to be prepared to defend yourself the whole time you are engaged with the interviewer. Otherwise, you may achieve a near-perfect performance with one fatal mistake.

Hot-topic questions. You may have parts of your history that you'd rather no one knew about—bankruptcy, substance abuse, a nasty divorce, cancer, prison time. Some of these facts may be public information that is easily accessible in a background search. So, even though you may have triumphed over some earlier problem, naturally you fear that the topic might arise. You can't rewrite your life, but you can avoid getting knocked out by something that happened long ago.

"Gotcha" questions. Interviewers often place more confidence in adverse information because they feel that it is more believable, so they adopt a favorite question to expose a negative. If you respond with negative information, the interviewer rates you down; but, if you respond with a positive, the interviewer continues to scan for negatives. This sequence can become a relentless witch hunt that ends only when you give up some bad stuff. But it's risky to give up a negative to this interviewer.

Questions out of your experience. If you're a recent college graduate, you may have very little work experience to draw on to answer questions, or you may be asked about technical skills that are not yet in your repertoire. You can recognize these questions because you don't need time to think of an answer—you know you don't have one—and if you aren't careful to compensate for your lack of experience, the interviewer will score the question against you.

Double-trouble questions. This kind of question is actually very clever; the interviewer poses a question which, when answered, will provide negative information about you. For example: "When have you found it necessary to put your work over your family?" or "What would you do if you suspected that your best friend at work was using sick days to add to vacation time?" You can get into trouble no matter how you answer.

Questions for negative information. These questions are asked by well-trained interviewers to get a representative sample of positives and negatives in your skills. Often they are phrased as a reverse of information that you have already given. For example, "Describe a time when you put in extra effort to get a job done on time" might be followed by "Now describe a time when you didn't work as hard as you should have." You don't want to pretend you're perfect—do you?

YEAH-BUT: It seems you are asking me to be a chameleon, changing my colors based on the question I am asked. I prefer to give my true answer, regardless of who asks it. I am who I am.

COACH'S COMEBACK: I admire your desire to be truthful, but I am not asking you to be dishonest. I'm showing you how to phrase your answers to protect yourself from an interviewer who is subjective, biased, and manipulative. Rather than a chameleon, I want you to be a butterfly. You went through a phase when you were less than attractive, but now you are transformed, a beautiful, admirable creature who can carve a path expertly on the breeze.

. . . AND OVER HERE, KID DYNAMITE

You can handle killer questions using the techniques on the following pages. Each is aimed at a particular kind of question, but the best way to use them is to find ways to combine them. They are:

- Highlight a compensating strength.

- Apply damage control.

- Show learning from mistakes.

- Disagree tactfully.

- Dilute the negative.

- Admit that you are not perfect.

Once you understand the technique, select a question that relates to you and use the form to answer it.

RESPONDING TO ILLEGITIMATE QUESTIONS

Odds are that if you are interviewed more than a few times you will be asked at least one question that could be subject to legal scrutiny. When it happens, respond in a way that maximizes your chances of getting the job, or at least minimizes the damage coming from the question. Your first impulse may range from challenging the interviewer directly to breaking off the interview and calling a lawyer. Of course you have the right, but you shouldn't take such a move lightly. Your anger may have faded, you may even have found a better job, long before the process has run its course. It's emotionally draining and expensive, it distracts you from your job search, and the results may disappoint you. Only one person is assured of employment—your lawyer.

You can respond to an illegal question is many different ways. Each entails a different combination of risk and opportunity. Refusing to answer is the riskiest tactic; although it's not as confrontational as reacting with overt anger or taking the organization to court, it can put a stop to unfair questioning. However, I know of few candidates who have advanced in the screening process by refusing to answer illegal questions.

Thoughts:

HIGHLIGHT A COMPENSATING STRENGTH

When the interviewer asks you to talk about one of your weak points, answer honestly, and follow through by highlighting a strength that compensates for the weakness. Show that you can recognize your own failings and learn from them. Give an example of a situation in which you made a mistake but used another skill to accomplish the same objective, limit the damage, or even improve the outcome. If you acknowledge that you're less than a top-notch organizer and planner, emphasize that you compensate for it with high skills in following policy and procedures.

Sample Questions

"What is your weak point?"

"Are you more selfish, more hard-headed, or more disorganized?"

"Which of your values do you fail at the most?"

"Describe a time when your biggest weakness hurt your performance."

Answer Guide

1. State your area of improvement:

   "One of the characteristics I need to improve is _____."

2. Highlight a strength that will compensate for the weakness.

   "As I improve in this area, I try to use my skill in _____ to help me avoid making any big mistakes."

3. Describe a past event that shows how you successfully used a strength to compensate for your weakness.

   "Let me give an example that relates to this issue.

   "The situation involved _____.

   "I was hindered by _____.

   "The actions I took were _____.

   "The result was _____.

   "I would evaluate the results by saying that _____
   _____."

4. State your conclusion about yourself.

   "My conclusion is that I am _____
   _____."

APPLY DAMAGE CONTROL

Even if you are a very skilled individual and highly qualified for the job, you may have a serious problem or character-related shortcoming in your past—bankruptcy, termination for cause, DWI conviction—that you have overcome and would rather not dwell on. However, the interviewer may have documented evidence of it and may be very direct about wanting to discuss it with you. You can reduce the impact by showing, with humility, how you have learned from the experience. If the negative was the result of a character defect, show that you have changed for the better. Say that you are committed never to make that mistake again. In general, don't volunteer information about your past difficulties, but don't try to hide them if you are asked directly about them.

Sample Questions

"What do you consider the biggest screw-up in your life?"

"How has your self-esteem been set back by a negative experience?"

"What would you like to change about your past?"

"When did you disappoint yourself at work by not following your principles?"

Answer Guide

1. Reflect humility.

   "This period of my life had some things about it that I'm not very proud of. At that time I had a problem with _____."

2. "Let me give an example that relates to this issue [make this extremely short].

   "The situation involved _____ .

   "I was hindered by _____.

   "The actions I took were _____.

   "The result was _____.

   "I would evaluate the results by saying that _____
   _____."

3. State your conclusion about yourself.

   "My conclusion is that I am _____
   _____.

   "I feel a great deal of optimism about the future. This is because I _____
   _____."

SHOW LEARNING FROM MISTAKES

An interviewer may, with or without evidence, ask you to identify and discuss a mistake you made on the job. You can turn this question to your advantage by telling what went wrong and what you learned from it. Support your answer with an example of a time when you used what you learned from the experience. Be specific; show that you can identify mistakes and convert them to principles that you can apply in other situations.

Sample Questions

"In what ways have you been too easy on people?"

"How has your sensitivity caused you to be less effective?"

"How do you feel about being yelled at?"

"Describe a time when you were not effective in managing conflict at work."

Answer Guide

1. Describe how you recognized the mistake, hopefully before others saw it.

   "When dealing with _____ , I focused on being direct and reasonable."

2. Describe reasonable actions you took or planned to take.

   "In this situation, I was reasonable in what I did because_____
   _____."

3. Describe what you learned from the experience.

   "I applied what I learned in a new situation. This situation involved _____
   _____.

   "I was hindered by _____.

   "The actions I took were _____.

   "The result was _____.

   "I would evaluate the results by saying that _____
   _____."

4. State your conclusion about yourself.

   "My conclusion is that I am _____
   _____."

DISAGREE TACTFULLY

The interviewer may have certain negative assumptions about you or may draw incorrect negative conclusions from one of your answers: "I understand that the position you held in your last organization was considered a low-skill job," or "From what you've just told me, there are times you're not as disciplined as you should be." You can counter inaccurate conclusions by tactfully disagreeing with the interviewer's interpretation: "I can see how you might draw that conclusion, but I have to disagree. I may seem unconcerned with minor points, but I'm very disciplined on the important parts of my job. For example. . . ."

Sample Questions

"You have limited leadership experience. Why should I give you a chance?"

"You seem to be too nice to be a good leader. Can you prove me wrong?"

"You just don't have the skill needed to lead this team."

"When were you unhappy with your leadership effectiveness?"

Answer Guide

1. Recognize the interviewer's reasoning by restating key parts of the question.

    "I can see the reasoning behind your question. You are saying that _____
    _____."

2. Say that you can't agree with all of the interviewer's reasoning.

    "On the other hand, this is a very complex topic and I can't agree that _____
    _____."

3. Give an example from your past to make your point.

    "For example, when I worked at _____, I dealt with a situation in which _____.

    "I was hindered by _____.

    "The actions I took were _____.

    "The result was _____.

    "I would evaluate the results by saying that _____
    _____."

4. State your conclusion about yourself.

    "My conclusion is that I am _____
    _____."

DILUTE THE NEGATIVE

Remember that the interview is not a career-counseling session. Although it's best to be honest, the interviewer may start to overemphasize a negative bit of information. Admit that you're not perfect, then move on quickly to your assets. Accentuate the positive by following the 5/55 rule: admit your negative in 5 seconds, then spend the next 55 seconds talking about your more positive attributes. "Yes, I have to admit that I'm sometimes impatient with people. But I think in the long run this works to the customer's benefit, because I'm impatient with co-workers who don't follow customer-oriented procedures. When I worked at XYZ, I had to tell one co-worker that. . . ."

Sample Questions

"People say that you are weak on detail. How do you respond to that?"

"Do you have the fortitude to break a stupid policy when necessary?"

"How do you feel about following procedures that slow down your work?"

"When have you not followed a procedure that you should have followed?"

Answer Guide

1. Briefly recognize the negative.

    "There could be a pretty negative outcome if I _____
    _____."

2. Provide at greater length a positive example that honestly minimizes the negative.

    "On the other hand, I know that _____.

    "Let me give an example that relates to this issue. The situation involved
    _____.

    "I was hindered by _____.

    "The actions I took were _____.

    "The result was _____.

    "I would evaluate the results by saying that _____
    _____."

3. State your conclusion about yourself.

    "My conclusion is that I am _____
    _____."

ADMIT THAT YOU ARE NOT PERFECT

To acknowledge imperfection is simply to be realistic. It shows the interviewer that you have a firm grasp of reality, that you know you're human and fallible. Do not, of course, volunteer your shortcomings in response to every question. Keep in mind that you want to be competitive. But when asked about your negatives, you can describe yourself as a work in progress and state that you enjoy the process of continuous self-improvement.

Sample Questions

"It sounds like you run from problems. Why can't you tackle things head on?"

"What is the biggest flaw in your personality?"

"How have your principles failed you regarding job stress?"

"When were you not successful in coping with a pressure situation?"

Answer Guide

1. Acknowledge that you are not perfect.

   "I have to admit that I am not perfect. One of my areas for personal growth involves _____. I am committed to continuous self-improvement. When I discover an area where I need personal growth, I develop a plan to use one of my strengths to help me improve."

2. Give an example that shows that you are constantly learning.

   "The situation involved _____.

   "I was hindered by _____.

   "The actions I took were _____.

   "The result was _____.

   "I would evaluate the results by saying that _____
   _____."

3. State your conclusion about yourself.

   "My conclusion is that I am _____
   _____."

THE JOY OF SKILLFUL EVASION

Some candidates, when asked blatantly illegal questions, manage to answer with humor and divert the interviewer's attention from the topic. If you're good at thinking on your feet, you may be tempted to do likewise, and you may be successful in deflecting the bias in the question. But be warned: some interviewers may consider you sarcastic or aggressive.

Q: "Mrs. Jones, tell me about your family."

A: "My mother takes care of our two children and my husband has had a vasectomy."

Q: "How will you feel when you make sales calls on white customers?"

A: "I'll feel proud of the quality product line I represent."

Q: "Do you regard yourself as being a person of color?"

A: "Yes. I qualify as an Equal Employment Opportunity statistic, in case you have an audit."

Q: "Do you go to church on Sunday?"

A: "It depends on how much I have to do at work."

Q: "Were your parents immigrants?"

A: "My father told me that everyone who's not an American Indian is an immigrant."

Q: "How old are you?"

A: "I'm old enough to appreciate the importance of doing a good day's work every day."

Q: "Do you have any health problems?"

A: "Yes. I'm a workaholic."

Another way to respond to illegal questions is to answer directly, then continue by addressing the interviewer's concerns and giving positive information about your skills. For example, the interviewer asks you, a female candidate, "How do you feel about latchkey kids?" You respond directly:

"I agree that young children need someone at home for them all the time. But my kids are older and they've learned how to take care of themselves. They know they can contact me or their father in case of emergency. They have become more responsible and self-reliant, and by being dedicated to my work, I'm giving them a good role model."

This answer deals with the concern of the interviewer, whether it is legal or illegal. Second, it lets you promote one of your performance skills—your dedication to your work. You could extend this answer by giving a SHARE example of a time when you successfully completed a crucial project while handling a minor domestic crisis. You could talk about other skills that you brought to the job, such as your ability to handle crises calmly and effectively.

THE WINNER, BY A DECISION

Dealing with negative information is tricky. The untrained interviewer tends to be suspicious of positive information—since it's obviously to your advantage to offer it—and thus tends to overreact to negative information, on the assumption that it is more accurate. A skilled interviewer, on the other hand, is more able to keep negative information in a realistic perspective.

Now that you've seen a few samples of how tough the questions can be, you may feel discouraged about getting out of an interview alive. So much information, so much to remember—by now you may have overloaded your circuits and tripped a breaker. But don't worry; if you've identified the negatives you're likely to be asked about and planned just a few responses, you're well equipped to answer a wide variety of other questions. You may find yourself using responses you've framed for these killer questions to answer positive questions as well. Once prepared, trust yourself.

COACH'S TIP: Practice, practice, practice! You cannot memorize your answers to killer questions and expect to deliver them convincingly. You must practice your answers—aloud! If you can arrange it, have someone ask you the sample killer questions and then critique the way you dealt with them.

Thoughts:

PART THREE

PRESENT YOUR CASE

You've done everything you can to prepare yourself for the interview. You've identified your skills, connected them with potential benefits for your employer, rehearsed answers to all kinds of questions, skill-related and otherwise.

By now you should be feeling fairly confident about the package of skills you are going to present to an interviewer.

An acquaintance of mine once told me, "I'm a whiz at getting ready for an interview. I write out and rehearse every major point I want to make, I get friends to ask me tough questions, I review every detail and all the facts and numbers I can think of. I'm ready for any question anyone could possibly ask me.

"But I stall out when I start talking to an interviewer. I've been calmer getting shot at in combat."

In that last sentence, my friend described the next challenge you are facing. Sure, you can plan and plan, but when it comes to the crunch, the worst time is after you've finished preparing and before you've begun to act. Sure, you know how to respond appropriately and well, but will you? Can you pull this off?

Then answer is yes—you will do fine. You will discover that when the interviewing process begins, all of your preparation will kick in.

The first step is the hardest—and the most important. Once you start contacting interviewers and responding to their questions, you'll find that your preparations will lead you to say the right thing at the right time.

Of course, you can never predict exactly what will happen when you get face-to-face. Each interview will have its own feel, its own energy, its own line of progress as it develops from moment to moment. There will be a unique mix of questions, responses, moods, prejudices, courtesies, and appearances.

That's what this next part of the book is about—the moment-to-moment dramatic action of the interview itself. You'll learn in chapter 9 that interviewing begins when you pick up the telephone. Whether you are sourcing interviews, coordinating interviews, or taking interviews, it's important to make the telephone your friend. Next, chapter 10 will show you how to cultivate one or more advocates to support you. Chapter 11 will explain how to establish and maintain an easy rapport. Chapters 12 and 13 will give you tips on how to avoid getting into trouble in the interview. When you are successful, you may be invited to visit with the corporate psychologist; chapter 14 will give you pointers on what to expect.

In earlier sections you did behavioral preparation: you practiced what to say and how. Now you're ready for mental preparation—getting your mindset right for the real thing.

9

BUILD YOUR TELEPHONE CONFIDENCE

When I was a child, I once asked my father how to hit a home run.

"Here is how to hit a home run," he said. "First, you have to show up for practice. Then, in the game, you pick up a bat and stand at the plate, ready to swing. You have to keep your eye on the ball. When you hit the ball, run as fast as you can to first base. If things are clear then you might be able to run to second base. Be alert while you are running around the bases. Sometimes you'll be able to run around all the bases, but that only happens once in a while. In order to hit a home run, you have to practice and be ready to swing at a lot of pitches."

At the time, I felt a little sorry that I had even asked the question. I didn't want to know that much about hitting home runs. But the message stuck with me: To get on base, you have to be able to swing the bat, hit the ball, and run.

The interviewing process begins when you pick up the phone to get on base. Are you clear, confident, and credible? "How did you get this number?" "Why are you taking up my time?" "Who are you, anyway?" These are all questions you don't want to have to answer, but you do want to see that they are answered by the way you use the telephone.

It all begins with the first call to set up an interview. You may have used e-mail to do your basic introduction; you may have sent an electronic résumé. But the first real challenge is to communicate well on the phone. Can you call and get an interview? Can you get an advocate to work for you behind the scenes? Can you be effective with a telephone interview, or even a video interview, before you sit down face-to-face with an interviewer?

Using the telephone effectively is a learnable skill. You may feel some level of telephone terror, but the key is not how you feel about the phone right now—it's what you learn to do with the telephone. With practice, one step at a time, you can become very good at communicating by telephone. And taking that first step can be very rewarding, as you will see.

TELEPHONE ROULETTE

Once, while serving as a consultant for a life insurance agency, I was asked to help a frustrated agent named Tom find another job. He really wanted to be a success in the business, but he just couldn't get on first base. As his manager put it, "In six months the only policy he sold was to his mother."

We began his job search by setting goals and developing lists of potential employers. However, after two weeks of list building, Tom had not turned up a single interview. Although he was bright and intellectually curious, he was more prone to contemplation than action.

My goal for our next meeting was to help him see the importance of taking action on his plans. When he arrived, I told him that we were going to do telephone prospecting.

First, I asked him to write a short guide to introduce himself and explain why he should get an interview. The guide was general enough to cover almost any situation, but specific about what he could do for an employer. We practiced with the guide until he felt he could talk naturally about its main points. Then we put it aside.

Next, I asked him to give me his trust—a "blank contract" based on my sincere interest in his success. I wanted him to try a novel approach that I believed would immediately get him interviews and reward him for taking action. He agreed. I explained that we were going to play "Telephone Roulette." Following my instructions, he flipped through the yellow pages at random and blindly put his finger on a company name. It was the name of a paint store. "Call and get an interview," I said. He seemed a little shocked, but he had promised to do what I asked.

Using his guide with practiced ease, he managed to arrange an interview for a supervisor's job in the paint store. He riffled through the yellow pages again and got a job referral from the attorney he had randomly selected. Then he called the metropolitan sports complex and got an interview with the City. Every time he called, he got results. He was amazed: "All I have to do is call!"

Tom soon realized that the purpose of Telephone Roulette was to show him that the telephone was his friend. We both recognized that making random

---

SIXTY-SECOND TELEPHONE GUIDE

1. Salutation (5 seconds).

   "Hello, I am _____. Thank you for the opportunity to speak with you."

2. Set the stage (5 seconds).

   "To refresh your memory, we met at _____."
   Or: "I was referred to you by _____. Is this a good time to talk?"

3. Establish the reason for the call (10 seconds).

   "I am calling about _____.
   I understand that you have an opening for a _____.
   Could you tell me what type of skills you're looking for?"

4. Establish your qualifications (15 seconds).

   "I have worked as a _____.
   I have experience in _____."
   My degree is in _____.

5. Make benefit statements (10 seconds to 2 minutes).

   "I am skilled in _____.
   I was trained in _____."
   I have completed classes in _____.

6. Ask for an interview (5 seconds).

   "I would like to ask for an interview. Is there a time that would be convenient to you?"

7. Wrap up the conversation (10 seconds).

   "Thank you for the opportunity of speaking with you. Is there anything special I should prepare to talk about in the interview? Can you give me directions to where the interview will take place? I'm looking forward to meeting with you."

calls was not the best way to get interviews. After he began a targeted calling plan, he was able to prospect for a job that would better fit his own needs. He got a good job offer within two weeks. When I saw him later, he told me that he was happy with his work and in line for a promotion.

CALL RELUCTANCE

Over the years I have worked with many people who suffered from call reluctance—salespeople who weren't realizing their potential and job search candidates who waited passively for opportunities, among others. Low self-esteem, fear of rejection, and other factors kept them from picking up the telephone and placing themselves in the way of opportunity. They rationalized their reluctance with any number of excuses.

A lot of people say they like talking with people but hate using the telephone. If you're this kind of person, you're hurting your job chances. Being able to use the telephone effectively is one of the most valuable career skills that you can have. The telephone is a contact multiplier: it lets you present yourself to many more people that you can talk with in person.

The more contacts you can make, the more high-potential interviews you will land. In a month of hard work, you can meet twenty people in person—or you can make 400 telephone calls. Learn to use it effectively, to state clearly how the organization can benefit by interviewing you face-to-face, and you will get interviews that will put you in opportunity's way.

YEAH-BUT: Forget it! I hate using the telephone.

COACH'S COMEBACK: Keep trying. It's a very important skill, and you can learn to do it well. Think of a time in your past when circumstances forced you to learn something; apply that understanding to your current situation. If you don't learn to be effective with the telephone, you will dramatically reduce the number of contacts that you can make. In a tight job market, someone who is willing to use the phone will get your job!

PHONE TO GET INTERVIEWS

How, you may ask, can I learn to use the phone the way the experts do, the ones who are successful at making all those contacts? The answer: Watch the pros. Visit a professionally managed customer-service call center—one that both receives calls from customers and makes telemarketing sales calls. Watch a service representative handle a customer or a prospect. Observe how his office is arranged, what resources and supplies he keeps at hand. You'll begin to understand what

THE WORLD'S GREATEST EXCUSES NOT TO CALL

- Someone may be trying to call me about a job.
- I need to eat first to build up my energy.
- I only have about twenty minutes.
- My dog is barking now.
- I already have an interview set up.
- I am going to wait and see if I get engaged.
- I want to loose five pounds before I interview.
- I haven't had a vacation in ten years.
- I am already too stressed out.
- I need to buy a word processor first so I can do letters.
- The interviewer is probably at lunch.
- The newspaper said that business was bad now.
- They wouldn't be interested in me.
- I don't want to work in that part of town.
- One of my friends already tried to get a job there.
- I need to get a haircut before I start interviewing.
- It's Friday afternoon—nobody will be there.
- I need to build my telephone file first.
- I don't have my stationary yet.
- I need to get a new suit.

---

you may be doing wrong, and you'll learn some telephone techniques that can help you get in for an interview.

Keep in mind that, for all practical purposes, the interview begins with your first telephone contact. Many interviewers will begin to rate your professionalism and interpersonal skills according to how well you conduct yourself on the phone. Take a hard look at your telephone skills, and prepare yourself to build a good first impression.

COACH'S TIP: Keep your résumé next to the phone. It will prompt you as you respond to questions, enabling you to be specific on your work history and skills.

WHAT TO SAY

How do you choose precisely the words to say over the phone that will win you an interview? Stay focused on one central fact: You must be prepared to help the recruiter believe that it is to her organization's benefit to grant you an interview.

Being prepared means not only being ready to communicate key facts about your qualifications, but also cultivating a telephone presence that is

- confident, but not arrogant.

- prepared, but not mechanical.

- professional, but not cold.

- assertive, but not aggressive.

- friendly, but not cavalier.

- available, but not needy.

For getting across your qualifications efficiently and effectively, there's no substitute for a telephone guide. Writing a guide makes you think about exactly what you wish to communicate. It can help you discover and avoid words or phrases that might give the recruiter the wrong impression. It helps you project a positive image of yourself, along with your summary of what you can do for the organization. Once you have developed and polished it, your telephone guide will give you confidence—a calm self-assurance that will help your contact realize you are the kind of person she wants to interview.

YEAH-BUT: There's nothing worse than hearing a canned script—you've been right on a lot of things, but this is bad advice!

COACH'S COMEBACK: Preparing a telephone guide stops before canning it. Actors use scripts very effectively. Every word is written out, internalized, and delivered with skill to reflect the role being played. Your role is to be an honest, effective job candidate who gets good interviews. This means learning what to say, practicing it, and feeling confident that you are a real person, not a robot. State the points in your guide aloud as many times as it takes you to feel natural.

Most contact calls last only a few minutes, just long enough for you to establish rapport, state your qualifications for the job, and arrange an interview, if possible. Your basic conversation needs to be to the point; don't try to keep the recruiter on the line longer than she wants. Sometimes, however, if you've raised the interviewer's interest, you may find your call turning into a telephone mini-interview. You need to be prepared for this contingency, ready to communicate on any aspect of your career, to describe such things as

- your educational experiences and special training.

- your employment history.

- the kinds of jobs you are qualified for.

- special qualifications for the job you are applying for.

- your knowledge of the organization's work.

- your understanding of the organization's culture and values.

There are many ways you can communicate these things on the telephone, some more effective than others. When you prepare for an in-person interview, you anticipate what you will be asked about and plan your response in the form of detailed skill-benefit questions. When you plan your first telephone contact with your target organization, you should also try to anticipate how the conversation will go but prepare to respond more succinctly. Formulate answers that are practical and to the point.

COACH'S TIP: Follow up after calls with a skill-based résumé—an explicit statement of what you have done in your career. This reinforces the skills you've described over the telephone and begins to demonstrate that you have a set of skills that are worth evaluating in a face-to-face interview. Many interviewers like to ask questions based on what they see on your résumé. The skill-based résumé makes it easy for the interviewer to ask about your skills and how they could be used in your new job.

Thoughts:

PREPARE FOR THE TELEPHONE INTERVIEW

Many organizations use a telephone interview as a standard part of the screening process. This use of the telephone goes well beyond the contact call, even the mini-interview call. A telephone interview covers much of the same territory as a traditional face-to-face interview. You may not meet an interviewer in person until late in the selection process, after you have been selected as a finalist.

YEAH-BUT: I hate the idea of a video interview. I don't look good on TV.

COACH'S COMEBACK: Well, make yourself look as good as you can look. Dress professionally, prepare to look at the camera when talking, and get the clutter out of the background. You can use a mirror to practice looking at the camera—just look at the tip of your nose and practice answering. Forget the "cutesy" stuff like a puppet show or funny hats. Just be professional and provide information that shows that you can do the job well.

From the employer's standpoint, the telephone interview is effective for eliminating unqualified candidates with minimal commitment of time and resources to assess their skills. It is also fast and easy to administer. The emerging technology of Internet video and video phones will make the telephone interview even more likely.

For the candidate, a telephone interview has its advantages and disadvantages. It can be unpredictable; you don't know when, or even if, you'll be called. The telephone rings, you answer, and you and the interviewer decide on the right time for the interview. With this format, it doesn't much matter whether you've shaved or put on makeup.

A telephone interviewer usually spends ten to thirty minutes asking questions about your education, job skills, technical knowledge, and work experience. This kind of interview typically puts the most emphasis on your technical proficiencies, because they are often minimum qualifications for the job. Competencies, such as teamwork, organization, and leadership, are more likely to be evaluated in person.

Once in a while you may experience an "ambush" interview. That is, the interviewer may try to catch you off guard to see how you respond to questions under pressure. I consider this a rather low-grade way to assess your job skills and would doubt the objectivity and competence of any interviewer using this technique. Nevertheless, prepare for an ambush interview the same way you would prepare for a professional telephone interview.

- Organize your household so you can control who answers your phone. Do not allow children or adults with unprofessional telephone presence to answer your line.

SAMPLE TELEPHONE INTERVIEW QUESTIONS
FOR A BOOKKEEPER IN A REAL ESTATE COMPANY

- What aspects of your work experience would relate to bookkeeping for a real estate company?

- What experience have you had with double-entry bookkeeping?

- How often do you need to reconcile depreciation schedules with your balance sheet?

- What types of accounting information should you immediately report to your manager?

- What types of accounting software packages do you have experience with?

- What experience have you had in reconciling multiple bank accounts?

- What experience have you had in reading amortization schedules?

- Describe the key aspects of planning that a bookkeeper should carry out.

- Describe the payroll procedures you've worked with.

- What is the bookkeeper's role in maintaining rental records?

- Tell me how to develop financial statements that account for assets, liabilities, revenue, and expenses.

- How do you develop quarterly payroll tax forms?

- Explain the procedures for administrating medical and disability insurance.

- Describe how to maintain retirement plans.

- What information should the bookkeeper compile for the tax accountant?

- To prepare for a video telephone interview, dress as you would if you were face-to-face. Remove visual clutter and have a solid background behind you.

- Use an answering machine or caller I.D. to screen your calls. Answer calls from the recruiter or an interviewer immediately.

- Keep your résumé and copies of all correspondence near the telephone so you can refer quickly to information you sent the employer.

- Breathe deeply before you pick up the phone. Excitement or running to the phone can make you short-winded.

During the telephone interview, be as specific as possible in answering questions. Prepare by formulating SHARE answers, just as you would for an in-person interview. On the phone, you have an extra advantage: you can keep a crib sheet handy to help you remember all the wonderful answers that you might have forgotten in a regular interview. Don't read them over the phone, through; just use them to jog your memory, then talk as though you were looking the interviewer in the eye.

> **COACH'S TIP:** Use the telephone to acquire advocates. The telephone is an essential tool in helping you recruit and maintain advocates who will work behind the scenes to facilitate your interviews. Sure, e-mail works, direct mail works, sending a résumé works. But the telephone is still the best way to ask for help in your job search.

One final point about telephone talk: never assume that you know what's happening on the other end of the line. While you're sitting there disheveled in your coffee-stained T-shirt, you may think you're having a heart-to-heart chat with a person who looks a lot like you and shares your feelings and beliefs. In truth, your remarks may be overheard by any number of people who happen to be near a speakerphone, some of whom may take offense at your witty remark about "empty suits" at work.

BEHIND-THE-SCENES HELP

It's reasonable to say that you need as much advance good will as possible to smooth your way into a favorable interview. You've done a lot to get things pointed in the right direction—identified the skills you have to offer, converted them to skill-benefit statements, and prepared SHARE examples. Then you charmed everybody with your easy telephone manner. You've already gone a long way toward getting prepared; the next chapter will help you arrive as you explore how to cultivate your advocate.

Thoughts:

10

CULTIVATE
YOUR
ADVOCATE

In my years as an interviewer, I considered it to be part of my job to protect candidates and organizations from partisan politics—that is, I was there to help select the most qualified candidate regardless of personal connections or biases. Nevertheless, I soon became aware of how often the candidate's success depended on behind-the-scenes advocacy. I came to understand that the advocate can do a great service for both the employer and the candidate by matching a highly qualified person with a crucial employer need.

Your advocates can be people on the selection team, elsewhere within the organization, or even outside the organization—in any case, people whose reputation, credibility, and influence can sway the decision in favor of hiring you. Advocates must know your skills and character and be able to describe what you could do for the organization. They can speak for you when you're not there, answer questions about you, and help communicate important information about your skills.

School ties have long been a natural source of advocates. Pledges to college fraternities and sororities are assigned "big brothers" and "big sisters" to speak up for the pledge in members-only meetings. A candidate for a university teaching job is typically brought to the faculty's attention and introduced by a champion who knows the individual's work. An advocate for a corporate job candidate is often someone who went to school with the candidate and can speak for the candidate's skills, potential, and work habits. You should consider every training experience an opportunity to find advocates for yourself as well as to become an advocate for others.

Of course, any behind-the-scenes subjective input into the selection process is vulnerable to abuse. A real problem with advocacy is that it can be discriminatory. The phrase "old boys' club" comes to mind. When the most powerful advocates share the same values and experiences, capable people with different backgrounds tend to be ignored, or worse, excluded. Taken to extremes, ardent advocacy can place people in positions for which they are not suited; the result can be disaster for both the organization and the employee.

COACH'S TIP: Recruiting advocates is a high-level sales skill; it's called "getting your foot in the door." Access to inside information—a client's needs, the likes and dislikes of a buyer, even past experiences with a competitor—sets the stage for closing the sale.

You also need to be aware that using an advocate can sometimes backfire. Your advocate may be using your candidacy as a way to deal with internal issues or a loss of credibility. Be alert to these possibilities; exercise your judgment. Don't let yourself be used as a political tool by others.

HOW TO ACQUIRE ADVOCATES

If you don't know anyone in the organization you're trying to get hired into, how do you identify someone who could become your advocate? It's not as hard as you might think. In a way, this question is backward. When you're scouting out employment prospects, sometimes it works better to think in terms of an advocate first, the organization second. That is, if you can first get in touch with an individual who is impressed by your credentials or otherwise favorably inclined toward you, that person may be able to steer you to a good

COACH'S TIP: Sometimes it's called politics, sometimes it's called an "inside track," sometimes it's called "networking"—but it's always smart to have a good behind-the-scenes advocate, someone who can help identify what jobs fit you best, who should interview you, and what you should emphasize.

job opportunity and help you maneuver through the process of getting an interview and a job offer.

Acquiring advocates is really an extension of identifying people you know who may be willing to help you. With this in mind, use a two-step approach. Ask, "Will you help me by. . . ." followed by a specific request:

"Will you help me by

. . . asking about openings at _____?"

. . . calling _____ and introducing me?"

. . . taking my résumé and cover letter to _____?"

. . . checking your phone list for possible contacts?"

If you ask for help, you improve the odds that you will get it. By adding a specific to the request, you are showing your advocate exactly what to do.

Most people like to be helpful. They feel good when they can be a positive in another person's life. So, by making the request, you are not only getting the help you need, you are also contributing to another's good feelings.

Start with Who You Know

The most efficient way to gain advocates is to contact people you have met, communicated with, or come to know in your work.

- Review the business cards you've saved over the years. Contact each person with the objective of gaining job leads.

- Compile a list of vendors and suppliers you have worked with in your jobs. Call and ask for ideas on places that need your skills.

- Contact a former employer or co-worker whom you pleased, and ask for an interview. If an interview is not forthcoming, ask for referrals.

- Use your time after working hours and on weekends to do contract work with business associates and prospective employers, taking care that there is no conflict of interest.

YEAH-BUT: Do I just ask somebody to be my advocate? That seems awfully pushy.

COACH'S COMEBACK: It can sound pushy if you don't test for willingness. Your best approach is to identify potential advocates and ask them questions about the job, the organization, and the organization's products or services. If the individual begins to give you encouragement, you have a possible advocate. If you don't get much response, keep looking.

- Volunteer to do unpaid work for professional associates who might be interested in hiring you later.

Broaden Your Circle of Professional Contacts

After you have gotten in touch with people you know professionally, expand your efforts to include individuals you have not met but who might know of your work, who work in the same field as you, or who might otherwise be interested in your professional qualifications were they to learn of them.

- Use the *Wall Street Journal* and other business publications to develop a list of companies with a high price/earnings ratio. These are probably high-growth organizations that are actively recruiting candidates for a variety of jobs. Find the names of key people in these organizations.

- Go to the reception area of an organization you would like to join and ask for a recruiting professional by name. Indicate that you would like to wait until you can personally give him or her a résumé. Then go from there in building a relationship.

- At a meeting of a professional organization, ask the program chairperson to let you make a twenty-second announcement of your availability. When the time is right, stand up and introduce your skills to the audience.

- Most professional organizations have employment or placement services at their national conventions. Put yourself on the "available for interview" list, attend the convention, and meet employers.

YEAH-BUT: I see no reason why someone would want to be my advocate.

COACH'S COMEBACK: Well, you will probably never really know why advocates go out of their way for your benefit. But advocates do profit from helping you. They may

- need your help in their next job search.
- want you to take a job that supports their bonus.
- get a cash or other incentive to bring in recruits.
- look forward to you as their next boss.
- have a personal conviction to help anyone in need.

Don't worry about why someone may help you. Concentrate on getting helped.

- Take out an advertisement in your professional association's newsletter. Include a brief description of your education and skills and ask for an interview.

- Use your Internet contacts software to get people who know you well to give you an online testimonial. Then ask for additional support.

- Take part-time work in a temporary placement firm, and impress an employer well enough to earn an interview for full-time employment.

Recruit Advocates Outside Your Professional Circle

There are key individuals in influential positions who became successful because they are helpful people. These may be people you do not know personally and who are not associated directly with your professional interests, but who may nevertheless be motivated to help you find employment opportunities.

- Write to your congressional representative, explaining what you do and where you would like to work. You will receive a call from a congressional aide who can be very helpful.

- Arrange for an interview with your banker. Present your résumé, review your skills, and ask for interview leads, with a personal introduction if possible.

- Ask a stockbroker who is selling securities in your field. Then ask if he or she can help you get an introduction.

COACH'S TIP: Assume that busy people in responsible jobs do have the time to help you. Successful people typically return their calls and respond to inquiries. You may, of course, get only a referral to another part of the organization, but that referral can open a door for you.

Reconnect Your School Ties

The schools you've attended can be a rich lifetime source of contacts. I've heard graduates from the most prestigious universities say that the greatest benefit of the schools they attended was the doors they opened. Not only do they get good interviews when they graduate, they can also recruit classmates or alumni to be their advocates.

- Using your high school and college yearbooks, develop a list of people to call. The odds are you know several successful people who will be glad to help you.

- Contact your favorite college professor(s), discuss your work experience, and ask for referrals to employers. A personal introduction by the professor is of great value.

- List yourself on a "classmate" website and scan for advocates.

- Attend the alumni association meetings; if possible, attend the homecoming.

- Contact your college placement officer. This person can often help you long after your graduation.

- Take evening classes to improve your professional skills. Ask the instructor and classmates for interview leads.

Mass Market Yourself

Another way to approach the problem is to think the way major merchandisers do. Communicate with people you know outside of work, or even people you do not know but who share some potential common interest. The more people you can contact, the more interviews you'll get. Sure, you may get responses from only a small percentage, but a fraction of a large number can be enough to give you a choice of several opportunities. Once you have an entrée into the organization, you can begin to cultivate advocates.

- Put your résumé on several Internet search boards and other emerging online services.

- Get a listing of government job openings. Complete all the paperwork for your application and be prepared to wait.

- Drive down the busiest street in your town. Make a list of the businesses that seem to be successful and contact them.

- Walk through a local shopping mall and identify the products and

---

YEAH-BUT: I feel that mass marketing myself is too impersonal. I just don't believe that it works.

COACH'S COMEBACK: Wrong! Mass marketing can work for you. I once conducted a seminar for thirty-two recruiters who fill 3,000 positions a year for one organization. They use every source available—the Internet, professional associations, newspaper ads, résumés, and referrals. Mass marketing only has to work once to be effective for you.

companies that seem to do well. Contact the successful organizations that appeal to you.

- Contact each person on your holiday mailing list. Ask for referrals for the specific type of job you are looking for.

- Call selected neighbors, explain that you are out of work, and ask for interview leads.

- Ask the people in your exercise or cooking class for referrals. This may steer you to opportunities outside your current business network.

- Display your résumé on the bulletin board at your child care center. Have your business cards tacked under your résumé to make it easy for someone to call.

FINDING YOUR CHAMPION

Following are some accounts by people of diverse backgrounds who have told me of their real-life experiences in cultivating advocates. These stories are very revealing; every person I asked was able to recount a positive experience—even people from groups that are regularly discriminated against.

> I got to know the placement officer in my college fairly well because we took classes together. When I graduated I didn't have a clue about where I could get a job. So my placement officer gave me the name of the recruiter for the convention bureau and told me that I must speak to this person. I was so persistent in calling that I thought, This lady is going to strangle me for bothering her. But I learned to get my message in quick. Eventually, the recruiter referred me to where I work today. She said that I was persistent and that seemed to be a plus—but the real thing is that she was willing to speak for me and persuade the company to interview me. —S. K.

COACH'S TIP: Make the advocate look good. We're all familiar with the idea of going out on a limb for another person, but it can be easy to forget that another person may have taken some risks for us. Remind yourself that you want to make the advocate feel proud of supporting you. Be polite, say please and thank you, watch your language, be on time, conform to the employer's culture. When you make the advocate look good, you reinforce his own judgment in supporting you, as well as his stature in the eyes of the selection team and of his employers. If you make the advocate look bad, then you look horrible!

I applied for a job, took a battery of tests, and completed a one-and-a-half-hour interview. I was told that I would know something within a week. When I didn't get a call, I went ahead and took another job. It was really bad. The second day on my new job I got a call to come in for my second interview at the place I wanted to work. The person who called me remembered who I was and became my secret advocate. He was able to explain to everyone why I should still be interviewed. This is where I work today. —W. S.

My job was eliminated just before I had my second child, so my severance package allowed me to take about eight months off work. Instead of taking a full-time job, I started taking job assignments with a temporary placement firm. They sent me to all kinds of places. It really gave me a complete view of what the job market was like for my skills. Then I was recruited to accept a full-time job by the person I worked for at my last assignment. He was my advocate to his boss, who had the final decision on hiring me. After I got the job, he told me that he liked to hire people based on their performance as a temporary. —A. B.

After leaving the air force, I completed commercial flight training. But I decided not to pursue an airline job because they wouldn't be hiring for some time. When I was being considered for a security director position, I discovered that the hiring manager had also been in the air force. That worked to my benefit. But the big advantage came because I was able to get a colonel who knew my work to call for me. He was the best advocate I could have asked for. I got the job with lightning speed. —G. W.

When I found that my department at the bank was to be eliminated, I went through the yellow pages and found the names of potential employers in my field. When I started making calls, I had my little speech set up—it was quick and clean. One of the people who returned my call explained that he knew that he was overdrawn and that it was already taken care of. When I explained why I was calling, we both had a big laugh. Then I got an interview and the job I have had for eight years. —A. P.

THE POWER OF PREPARATION

There are many, many ways you can access and benefit from advocates. The odds are that reading and following through on this information will make you think of many other resources I've failed to mention—resources that you alone would know about. Pursue every idea. Even a blind alley has an end, and you may meet someone there who has gone the same way and learned something he can teach you.

You have now made all the basic preparations you need for maximizing your chances of success in an interview. From now on, it's reality time. What do you need to say and do when you get in front of an interviewer? Do you offer to shake hands? What about your body language? Do you need a refresher on interview manners? Is there something you need to avoid saying? Don't worry, all of this will be covered in chapter 11, Building Rapport.

Thoughts:

Thoughts:

11

BUILDING
RAPPORT

The interviewer strides into the room and sits across the table from you. "Just who are you, anyway?" he demands.

Are you in the wrong room? Are the police on the way? Are your pants on backward? Who is this hostile person, and how are you supposed to respond to him?

Perhaps some of these questions went through the mind of the unfortunate candidate who was actually confronted this way. It startled me, too, and I was just there to observe. I had underestimated just how bad an untrained interviewer, even an intelligent and successful sales manager, could be.

Rather than attending a regular workshop, the interviewer had retained me to spend the day observing him, giving him feedback, and demonstrating my approach to interviewing. I pulled no punches. I told the interviewer that his technique was haughty, abrupt, and presumptive. It would made a good candidate regret showing up and put the average candidate on the defensive. It was a bad question, I said, and a bad way to start the interview. What was the value of being so abrupt with the candidate?

The interviewer explained that, in his opinion, an effective salesperson had to be able to "think on his feet." The "stress question" was meant to test the candidate's ability to deal with unruly customers—the way the interviewer had learned to do. A good salesperson should be able to shrug off rude, offensive comments, to "get the business, whatever the circumstances"—like the interviewer.

This interviewer was making the "cloning error"—looking for someone like himself in the belief that his way was the only way. Not only was his personal theory a poor basis for evaluating a candidate, it led to a disastrous beginning for an interview. It set a confrontational tone from the start, a move that immediately put the candidate on the defensive, killed rapport, and made it more difficult to get objective information about his real qualifications.

You may walk into the interview and find yourself facing just such an unpromising beginning. If you do, treat it as a test of your interpersonal skills. Stay calm. Take a beat or two. Think carefully about your answer. Look the interviewer in the eye, smile, and reply with a few well-chosen words. The way you take command of the situation will not go unnoticed; in fact, it may be exactly what the interviewer is looking for.

COACH'S TIP: Don't forget to smile. You may be the kind of person who wears a concerned, serious look when dealing with something as weighty as an interview. By smiling, at least upon first meeting the interviewer, you can contribute to rapport.

Good rapport progresses through three phases: attaining, maintaining, and sustaining. Attaining rapport takes only a few minutes, but it's an important few minutes. Your goal is to create a positive first impression by how you look and act, and to follow the interviewer's conversational lead. The rapport you build in the first phase tends to set, like gelatin. Maintaining rapport then becomes mostly a matter of avoiding big mistakes that can shatter the mold and turn off the interviewer. Sustaining rapport is mainly the task of finishing the interview gracefully and leaving behind a good impression.

ATTAINING RAPPORT

This first stage of rapport building lasts only five minutes or so (my rule of thumb), but the result, whether successful or unsuccessful, usually dominates the rest of the interview. Obviously, getting off on the right foot is your immediate goal. If you do, maintaining rapport is easier; if not, you spend a lot of energy trying to dig yourself out of a hole.

First Impressions

One way or another, you're going to make a first impression. Make it work for you, not against you. The car you arrive in, the shoes you're wearing, the way you walk into the room, your first remark—all convey a certain nonverbal impression to the interviewer. Make it a positive one; mind the details.

Research suggests that interviewers tend to search for negative information and come to quick conclusions about candidates based on information presented early in the interview. In one early study, 85 percent of interviewers' decisions were based on information from the first four minutes of the interview. A single unfavorable rating led to a rejection decision 90 percent of the time.

These results lead to clear recommendations. Pay particular attention to how you look, what you do, and what you say on first meeting the interviewer. Use common sense; interviewers and organizations differ, and standard rules may not apply. You won't always be expected to wear a business suit; offering a handshake could be a mistake. For each interview situation, make a conscious choice about how to present yourself.

Of course, a well-trained interviewer will avoid making snap decisions, but you can't count on having a good interviewer. Your best strategy is to prepare for the worst and consider yourself lucky if you draw a skilled interviewer.

Positive Visual Impact

Within the first few seconds of meeting the interviewer, you have already communicated a visual message. If you've prepared yourself well, your message will be that you are a skilled professional and a good team player with the skills for doing the job well. This message is more likely to be communicated if you

- inspect yourself before the interview by looking in a mirror.

- check that buttons, zippers, belts, and laces are correctly deployed.

- carry a planning calendar or a small briefcase with work samples.

- have a résumé ready (not folded).

You don't have to be expensively dressed or really good looking. Just try to avoid distracting the interviewer with your appearance.

The Handshake

Should you offer to shake hands? The tradition has been to extend your hand and give a firm, confident handshake. But this may be the wrong approach in some situations. Some cultures view touching as too intimate. Many women consider a handshake too much of a male tradition. And some, like one interviewer I met, are concerned about germs:

I interview sixteen college students a day. Many of them don't carry handkerchiefs and sneeze on their hands. Odds are I'm going to be exposed to the flu several times during a recruiting week. Also, I don't want to give Candidate Six the germs from Candidate Five when I shake hands. So I generally try to avoid shaking hands by making an open gesture of where the candidate should sit. It doesn't work all the time, so I regularly wash my hands between interviews.

A handshake today is a judgment call. If the interviewer extends a hand, go for it. Otherwise, smile big and wait for the invitation to sit.

Your Positioning Statement

By arriving well groomed, professionally dressed, and on time, you've communicated a lot about yourself—and you haven't yet said a word. Your next move is to speak, to make a positioning statement. It includes three components: (1) the interviewer's name, (2) your appreciation for the interview, and (3) an indication that you're ready to cooperate.

LOOK AT YOURSELF IN THE MIRROR

Many years ago I interviewed a recent college graduate who was bright, candid, and charming, and well qualified for the job. At the time I thought it rare and refreshing to see all of these qualities combined in one person.

He was also very fortunate to have an interviewer who could look beyond his superficial appearance. His black shoes were muddy; his belt was brown; his suspenders had flowers; his tie was askew. He was in dire need of someone else's experienced eye.

When it came to first impressions, I used to try to be critical of myself as an interviewer and forgiving of the candidate. I strove to credit the content of candidate's answers and ignore subjective negative impressions. Still, I was bothered by this candidate's loose tie, mesmerized by the inch of shirt I could see above it.

I could ignore many of the details of his image. But I kept asking myself, Why didn't he look in the mirror before the interview? If he had, he might have done something to make himself look better.

This story ends happily. I overcame my reservations and recommended hiring him on the basis of his knowledge, skills, and intellect. The employer was astute enough to look beyond first impressions; the candidate was offered the job. But the outcome could have been very different with another interviewer or another organization. His failure to look at himself with a critical eye could have been an expensive career mistake.

Pick one of the following examples that feels close to what you would naturally say, and put it into your own words. Then practice it.

"Dr. Green, it's a pleasure to have this opportunity to be with you today. I'm especially eager to share my skills in _____ with you."

"Mr. Smith, thank you for allowing me to interview with you today. I want you to know up front that I am excited about letting you get to know me and my skills."

"Ms. Jones, I appreciate this interview. I will be as thorough as possible in responding to your questions."

It is usually best to first address the interviewer with Mr., Ms., or an academic title such as Dr. If the interviewer prefers to use given names, then she will invite you to do so.

Some Dos and Don'ts

The first moments of an interview are sometimes awkward; you don't know quite what to say, and if the interviewer doesn't put you at ease immediately with a bit of banter, you may be tempted to say the first thing that pops into your head. This can be a mistake. It's better to allow a little silence while you get comfortable and compose yourself. In any case, there are some things you probably shouldn't mention when the interview starts up:

- Don't ask about salary or benefits.
- Don't refer to problems finding the office.
- Don't speak negatively about travel arrangements.
- Don't ask if the weather is always this bad.
- Don't bring up who you know in the organization.

YEAH-BUT: One of my real strengths in my job search is the people I know. My contacts have a lot of pull in some big companies. You seem to be telling me not even to mention my contacts.

COACH'S COMEBACK: Not exactly. You're the best judge of whether it is to your advantage to drop a name or two. All I'm saying is that you need to be very careful with this approach; it can backfire. Instead, emphasize your skills, and if your contacts work to your advantage, they may be an added value in the interviewer's eyes.

- Don't say that you didn't get much sleep.

- Don't explain why you might do poorly in the interview.

- Don't volunteer why you lost your last job.

- Don't make reference to religion, politics, race, gender, age, or national origin.

- Don't try to butter up the interviewer by complimenting her appearance.

- Don't ask if you can show letters of recommendation.

- Don't make negative reference to anyone.

- Don't request refreshments that aren't offered.

- Don't inquire about lunch.

Having made your positioning statement, focus the conversation on the needs and interests of the interviewer:

"Where would you like me to sit?"

"Could you use another copy of my résumé?"

"I've brought samples of my work that might interest you."

"Do you have any concerns about special job or skill requirements that I can address?"

"If you need any extra time with me, I can be very flexible."

"Here's my business card for your future reference."

The way these statements are phrased may not be exactly your style, but they illustrate the basic idea—be humble and helpful.

MAINTAINING RAPPORT

If you've come safely through the first five minutes or so of the interview, you'll spend most of your allotted hour maintaining rapport—unless you mess up and wander into the interviewer's minefield. Every interviewer has one, and if you stumble across one of the triggers, you will find rapport suddenly withering, and you may not even know why.

Interviewers tend to overreact to negatives, and trivial things can sink you. Something in your attitude, an innocent remark, an unconscious personal habit can rub the interviewer the wrong way and override all the good rapport and your excellent credentials. Most of these minefields are known, so with a little study you can learn where they are and how to stay out of them.

Self-Aggrandizement

Many interviewers will give you ample opportunity to describe times when you used your skills successfully at work. Remember, though, that the interviewer may also want to evaluate your skills in teamwork and cooperation. If you dwell exclusively on your personal qualifications, you may seem self-absorbed. Downplaying your skills and successes often makes good sense; as a practical Texan once said, "The rooster who crows loudest gets the axe."

Acknowledge the contributions others have made to your successes. Avoid overusing the word "I"; substitute "we" wherever you can. This does not mean you should talk in generalities; the interviewer will want to know exactly what steps you took in each situation. But the interviewer knows that others contributed to a successful outcome, and you should show that you are aware of this by periodically recognizing that you were part of a team.

Low Confidence

Interviewing folklore holds that eye contact, a firm handshake, and erect posture are important signs of a candidate's self-confidence, social skills, and employability. In today's more sensitive, multicultural work environment, such indicators are questionable. Nevertheless, there is some merit in using them in moderation to demonstrate self-confidence without arrogance.

Don't try to stare down the interviewer, but make eye contact while talking to him; when thinking out responses to questions, however, the most natural thing to do is to look to the side or into the distance. Shake hands only if the interviewer initiates the gesture—but be ready for it, and don't hesitate. Maintain good posture, but don't get rigid; sit straight, relax, and be as natural as possible.

> **COACH'S TIP:** Don't smoke anywhere around interviewers or an employer's work site. Avoid alcohol except when others encourage you, and then drink only a little. Either tobacco or alcohol can cost you the best job you could ever have had.

Educational Arrogance

In my years of interviewing, I've met a graduate from a top business school who said that his M.B.A. was more valuable than a doctorate from a state-funded university; a candidate who based his purported intellectual superiority on a three-month executive development program; and several brand-new Ph.D.s who wished to be addressed as "Doctor." Such attitudes tend to leave experienced interviewers wishing the candidate had taken a course in humility.

You may be justly proud of your educational achievements; but this can be one of the triggers in your interviewer's minefield. Keep in mind that the interviewer may not have had your educational opportunities and may be sensitive about it. If you seem smug about your schools, degrees, and honors, you may gain a point or two on education but lose several on interpersonal skills.

Humor

Since good rapport can involve smiles, friendliness, and even laughter, it's easy to see how having a good sense of humor can help you communicate with the interviewer. However, some candidates try to project so much of their personality through humor that they forget the limits of good taste. Jokes that involve race, gender, national origin, religion, age, or disabilities are out of bounds. If you're tempted to tell a story with any of the above elements, stop yourself. Not only does such misuse of stereotypes reflect on your sensitivity and character, you may tread heavily on unseen toes without knowing it. Sacrifice your moment of humor for the dignity of others—and to stay out of a very hazardous part of the minefield.

Overtalking

It is possible to be too eager to communicate. I once asked a candidate a simple question, "What is your strong point?" and was inundated with a forty-five-minute list of his strengths—nine in all—with multiple examples of how he had used them in his former job. I tried several times to switch topics, but he persisted. I was unable to learn much of what I needed to know about him.

Most interviewers will see overtalking as self-indulgence, insecurity, or an attempt to control the interview. You should be alert to the interviewer's subtle clues and respond to her specific needs for information. If your answers

---

COACH'S TIP: You may encounter many situations when confidentiality rules what you say. For instance, your natural curiosity may turn up proprietary knowledge that you are not entitled to. The reverse is also true: you should not volunteer information or answer questions that reveal proprietary knowledge about your last employer. In either case, the interviewer may rate you low in integrity.

are too long and too detailed, the interviewer may, at best, think you cannot distinguish the important from the trivial; at worst, label you a "motormouth."

Money

Whether you're rich or poor, you have much to lose and little to gain in talking about money. The interviewer may entertain such thoughts as these:

> "He doesn't have to work."

> "Spoiled rich kid!"

> "If he's so broke, how did he buy that sports car?"

> "She's probably poor because she ignored her education."

Even if the interviewer reacts positively to the saga of your fortunes, it probably won't do much to land you the job. What's important is not what you have or don't have, but what you can do for the organization. Astute managers know that the best workers are those searching for job enrichment and job satisfaction, not money. Communicate your driving need for work that is stimulating and exciting, and don't talk about salary until later.

Names

"It's not what you know, it's who you know." Don't you believe it. With few exceptions, employers are more interested in hiring people who can help them compete in the cutthroat marketplace than in running a corporate country club. Trying to gain an edge by dropping names will make many interviewers think, Can't this guy make it on merit? Claiming to know top executives in the organization may even be perceived as a threat. One candidate I interviewed let me know, in a not terribly subtle way, that he was on a first-name basis with a former governor. I was less than impressed—I had voted for his opponent.

Eating

Many interviews, especially those with candidates on the short list, are conducted over dinner. Managers sometimes simply like to dine out at company expense, of course, but don't assume that what you say and how you behave are off the record. Although the interviewer may tell you that she simply wants to get to know you better, be assured that she has specific objectives to cover during dinner. She may want to see how you conduct yourself in a more relaxed situation, whether you know the difference between consommé and a finger bowl, how well you hold your liquor.

Table manners are a large part of the minefield; people grow up with different ideas of what constitutes good dining etiquette. Over the years, I've seen good candidates sink themselves by talking around mouthfuls of food, using knives and forks like weapons, sampling food from other peoples' plates, compulsively separating food into individual portions, and spilling their drinks. An interview over a meal provides hundreds of ways to get yourself evaluated on your eating habits rather than your skills. Keep in mind that your objective is to get hired, not to get fed.

Language

Here, in my opinion, is a firm rule: Never use profanity. Now, you and I both know people who habitually swear to emphasize a point; "It builds energy," they say. But many of us are more impressed by people whose command of the language can convey a message without profanity. An interviewer who hears you swear is likely to think one of two things about your vocabulary—either it is inadequate, or it is offensive. The trend today is toward more profane public language; resist it.

There is one other current movement that you should, however, pay particular attention to: nonsexist language. Don't describe people exclusively with male pronouns; it insults half of the human race. Some men shrug this off as trivial. Many women disagree. I once interviewed a trainer who had programmed himself always to use both masculine and feminine pronouns when saying such things as "If the manager discovers an integrity problem, he or she should take immediate action." I gave him extra points for that.

SUSTAINING RAPPORT

If you've established rapport with the interviewer, avoided the minefields, and then maintained rapport, all that's left is to leave with good feelings and without tripping over anything. You'll know when the end is near; the interviewer says something like, "Well, Jane, it looks like. . . ." or moves into "What's going to happen next" topics, or simply stands up and offers a handshake. This is your cue that you should prepare to exit.

Things have gone well; don't push it. Limit your questions and comments to these topics:

- Your understanding of the next step in the process

- A statement that you really want this job

- A "thank you" for the interview

That's it! Smile and leave the room as gracefully as possible.

MANNERISMS THAT KILL RAPPORT!

Do you know your rapport-killing mannerisms? Of course you do. They're the ones your parents, teachers, and significant others have been pointing out to you for years. The problem is not your lack of awareness, it's the way you rationalize your bad manners: "This is acceptable in Europe," or "Well, it's just mashed potatoes, and there's no ash tray. . . ."

The following exercise should show you where you need to make improvements in this area. Ask someone—a person you trust to tell you the truth—whether she has ever seen you exhibit the following mannerisms. Then ask whether the mannerism might hurt your image in an interview.

Mannerism	Observed		Image	
	Yes	No	Negative	Positive
Playing with hair	☐	☐	☐	☐
Biting nails	☐	☐	☐	☐
Coughing	☐	☐	☐	☐
Sneezing without a tissue	☐	☐	☐	☐
Avoiding eye contact	☐	☐	☐	☐
Snapping fingers	☐	☐	☐	☐
Slouching	☐	☐	☐	☐
Tongue thrusting	☐	☐	☐	☐
Popping knuckles	☐	☐	☐	☐
Licking lips	☐	☐	☐	☐
Cleaning fingernails	☐	☐	☐	☐
Picking nose	☐	☐	☐	☐
Pointing	☐	☐	☐	☐
Clenching teeth	☐	☐	☐	☐
Wringing hands	☐	☐	☐	☐
Putting hands to face	☐	☐	☐	☐
Crossing arms	☐	☐	☐	☐
Tapping pen	☐	☐	☐	☐
Picking at face	☐	☐	☐	☐
Playing with keys	☐	☐	☐	☐
Snorting	☐	☐	☐	☐

THE RAP ON RAPPORT

It's hard to get the toothpaste back into the tube, and it's almost as hard to over-come a bad first impression. I remember one applicant who disparaged a manager in his current organization, then, realizing that this made him sound judg-mental, tried to recover by explaining that his versatility had enabled him to work well with the manager. Unfortunately, this comment only made him seem insincere. He dug himself in deeper during the rest of the interview by refer-ring again and again to his versatility. Having made the original mistake, he compounded it by repeatedly bringing my attention to it.

Rapport is a two-way street, a measure of the good will and communi-cation between you and the interviewer that is almost an intangible. There is a more overt side to establishing and maintaining a good feel in the interview—a side that is your responsibility alone. As chapter 12 will show, your best bet is to get into the mainstream and stay there. It can easily make the difference between acceptance and outright rejection.

Thoughts:

STAY IN THE MAINSTREAM

All my life I've lived near the Mississippi River. From my current residence I can see the river churning past me, one mile wide and 100 feet deep.

I asked a retired riverboat captain to tell me about the river. I expected to hear about catching 200-pound catfish, or working the river in the '40s when he was a young deck hand. But he got a distant look in his eye, then looked right at me and gave me more than I expected.

"The currents in the river are powerful," he said, "but some of the most dangerous places are near the bank. Not just because you can be grounded. Near the bank whirlpools and eddies can suck a boat under and spit it up downstream in little pieces. At least in the mainstream you have a chance to stay in control and see the big debris coming toward you."

Good advice, I thought. Stay in the mainstream and make a safe trip.

And this is good advice for you: stay in the mainstream during your interviews. Tone down everything about yourself—except how your skills can benefit the employer. Forget the fact that you have a new motorcycle; don't talk about saving the whales or protecting the Amazon; fight the impulse to drop a few names; don't wear your most dramatic tie. Turn down the heat, except for what you can achieve at work. Become a black-and-white movie with one vivid, full-color scene: you, doing a good job.

Of course, I am overstating the importance of staying in the mainstream—but not too much. Consider the probability that some of the unique things about you will be seen by some interviewers as extreme. I recall a highly qualified Ph.D. who used the most outrageous profanity imaginable; a candidate who yelled at our receptionist; an interviewee who complained about tight shoes while rubbing her bare feet. They should have known better.

You, of course, would never make mistakes this big. But there are scores of things that you won't know not to do or say until it's too late. This chapter is about being on guard by taking the middle ground.

SHOW RESPECT

Since you can't know all the particulars in advance, the best way to begin to meet your prospective employer's standard of etiquette is to be conservative. Read the organization's annual report, prospectus, or mission statement for clues to this unwritten code of conduct. Network with friends and acquaintances to locate someone who works or has worked there. If you've already developed a good relationship with someone inside the organization—an advocate—don't hesitate to ask about any pitfalls that might not be obvious to an outsider.

THE BASIC INGREDIENTS OF EFFECTIVE IMAGE

- It's more than looks—actions count, too.

- The most effective image is the one held by leaders in your field.

- One detail askew can cause image confusion.

- Don't look too good—look professional.

- Don't "dress for success," dress for acceptance.

Be traditional in your social rituals, speech, dress, and manners. Think of yourself as having grown up on a farm in the Midwest among family who emphasized good manners by showing respect for the feelings and sensibilities of others. Address interviewers as Ms., Mr., or Dr. until invited to use first names—especially with a person of another race or culture. Stand when someone enters the room. Communicate clearly and with proper business English. Wait for the other person to offer to shake hands. Do all this as if it were your everyday custom; don't make it look as though you're doing something special for the interviewer.

THE MAVERICK IMAGE

I once heard an interviewer describe a candidate who was being considered for a high-tech position in a very conservative organization. Not only did the candidate show up without a tie, he wore sandals and sported a ponytail. When he walked into the room, everyone wondered what he had accomplished that allowed him to be such a nonconformist.

As it turned out, he possessed highly specialized technical knowledge that the organization needed badly. Because of his unique level of expertise and the overwhelming needs of the company, his eccentric self-presentation did not keep him from being hired.

Here is a checklist of achievements that, in most organizations, might entitle you to present a nonconformist image without denying yourself a shot at employment. If you can check yes beside any of these statements, consider yourself free to develop whatever image you want.

Yes	No	
☐	☐	I received a Nobel prize.
☐	☐	I am the principal contributor on 100 or more patents.
☐	☐	I was an effective and well-liked president of the United States.
☐	☐	I am a world expert on a billion-dollar technology.
☐	☐	I brought lasting peace to the Middle East.
☐	☐	I invented ten-calorie beer.

But what about the particulars? Some can, fortunately, be defined in advance. Some topics and situations call for caution: certain personal preferences, legally protected topics, dining with interviewers, and many more. These we will deal with in more specific terms, because many a promising career has been thwarted by a seemingly trivial error.

Perhaps you're the kind of person who feels a need to express individuality through language and dress. You're perfectly free to look and act as you wish, of course, but you may be working at cross-purposes with your career goals. What do you hope to gain from the interview—recognition, or a job? If it's truly the latter, concentrate on communicating what you can do, not who you are. Don't lead the interviewer to believe that you won't fit in with the rest of the team at work.

TICKLISH TOPICS

Let's begin with the obvious. It's not the topics you're sensitive about that matter, it's those that bother the interviewer. You will naturally refrain from talking about things that make you feel uncomfortable. But you will not automatically avoid topics that distress others.

When I was teaching classes in sales fundamentals, we discussed the importance of personal appearance in a sales presentation. One student, noticing that I had adopted a "clean" haircut to obscure the fact that I was balding, boldly asked me how I felt about toupees. My immediate reaction was to answer with a jest: "I obviously think that a toupee would make a man look worse, not better!" The class responded with laughter—except for one student. He was the one wearing a toupee.

My offhand response got a laugh and relieved some tension, but it also hurt another person. Had I known that he wore a toupee, I might have thought of the injury my remark would cause in time to stop myself. With more wisdom

---

IMAGE CONFUSION

Image confusion occurs when one aspect of a person's image is not in line with the rest. Here are some examples:

- an executive using a disposable pen to sign important documents

- a middle manager in a suit, with a tattoo coming up his neck

- an accountant with a ring in his ear

- a software engineer who wears an expensive watch but drives a beat-up car

Sometimes, of course, image confusion is the goal. Once, sitting in a downtown burger boutique, I saw two men ride up on expensive Harleys. Their clothes were clean, their nails manicured—but both had dirty faces. On closer inspection, I saw that they had achieved their stylishly incongruous look with the help of makeup.

There's a television personality who once drove an old, beat-up Checker taxi. The car had a high-performance engine, a lavish interior, a fantastic stereo system—but car thieves didn't give it a second look. If it got dinged, that was okay. And not incidentally, it added a little creative dissonance to the person's image.

For your upcoming job interview, though, avoid projecting image confusion. Most interviewers are confused enough as it is. Strive for consistency.

and faster reflexes, I might have redirected the question to the class and let them deal with it. Instead, my joke probably took me down a notch in another person's eyes. So, I adopted a rule: Never talk about toupees around strangers.

Some topics are too risky even to mention in an interview. Almost nothing you say about them can help you, and just bringing up the subject can hurt you. The following five are the most dangerous.

Sex

Make no reference to sex. Specifically:

- Do not tell jokes with a sexual content.

- Do not make comments about sexual preference.

- Don't say anything about sexual problems.

- Don't talk about sexually transmitted diseases.

- Don't discuss how any form of life reproduces.

- Don't describe any advertisement that uses sex to sell a product.

Think of yourself as a person in a Norman Rockwell painting. There are, of course, differences in the way males and females dress, but beyond that there is no sex in the painting.

Gender Stereotypes

Old stereotypes of the roles of men and women are as outdated—and sensitive—in the workplace as in society at large. Most issues at work concern discrimination against women: unequal compensation, stereotypical job assignments, sexual harassment. Often there is a "glass ceiling" that keeps women from moving into positions of authority. Although progress has been made, these issues are still being worked out in many organizations. The employer you are interviewing with may have had painful experiences that the interviewer does not wish to be reminded of.

Not all these issues are women's concerns. Some men complain about "male bashing," suggestions that they don't do their share of child care and

YEAH-BUT: I don't want to seem prudish. When I hear an off-color joke, I'm going to laugh.

COACH'S COMEBACK: The way you respond to one interviewer may be overheard by another who considers the joke offensive. Simply don't react to off-color comments. You'll be amazed at how others will change their behavior to meet your higher standard.

household chores, and reverse discrimination. It's not wise to assume that all men like sports, are fascinated by cars, and prefer action movies. Many men are sensitive to the feelings of others and can color coordinate their clothing.

You may feel that you have at times been the victim of sex-based stereotyping and discrimination. You're probably right. In the interview, though, you're well advised not to comment on these issues, casually or otherwise.

Race

Any competent interviewer knows not to use race as a basis for either selecting or rejecting a candidate. However, some interviewers and some candidates think they can show how open-minded and flexible they are, or at least get the subject out of the way, by talking casually or making friendly jokes about race. This doesn't work well; simply bringing up the subject demonstrates that you have some concerns about it. Although there may be some exceptions, the best rule is not to mention race at all.

> **COACH'S TIP:** Do yourself a favor: Don't say anything that reflects a stereotype about race, gender, color, religion, national origin, age, disability, or sexual preference. Many interviewers view these topics as highly personal matters that are completely out of bounds in the interview.

Here are some examples of things that you should not say:

"I'm good at working with people of all races."

"I am light-skinned, but I still count as an African American for your EEOC report."

"I have no problem working with whites."

"When it comes to customers, I work best with other Hispanics."

"Racism is alive and well in this country."

"Since you're Korean too, tell me about my opportunities in this organization."

Some would suggest that you can intimidate an interviewer into giving you a higher rating by making a point of the fact that you are in a racial minority. I do not feel that this is a good tactic. It may instead make the interviewer look for legitimate reasons not to hire you. Forget race. Showcase skills.

Social Standing

When talking to the interviewer about your skills, education, and job successes, you may find yourself edging into social standing, prestige, wealth, and contacts

CANDIDATE COMMENTS

Circle yes or no to indicate whether you believe the following comments are appropriate for a candidate to make. Compare your responses with the correct answers at the bottom of the next page.

1. Yes No   "I am Italian."

2. Yes No   "I have participated in six new-product rollouts."

3. Yes No   "I'm a Christian."

4. Yes No   "I earned my CPA last year."

5. Yes No   "I know a lot about your biggest competitor's product plans."

6. Yes No   "I always vote Republican."

7. Yes No   "I developed the outplacement program my last employer used."

8. Yes No   "I'm glad to see this organization has a policy on gay rights."

9. Yes No   "I was the only woman in a department of forty-two men."

10. Yes No   "I'm partially deaf, but I can do this job."

11. Yes No   "She has a great figure!"

12. Yes No   "I'm 64, so you can use my age for your government reports."

13. Yes No   "I have a master's degree in English."

14. Yes No   "I believe in not polluting the environment."

15. Yes No   "My last boss was a nut."

16. Yes No   "I am cured of cancer."

17. Yes No   "I'm an alcoholic. I've been sober for three years."

18. Yes No   "I have three children."

19. Yes No   "My father-in-law just won the lottery."

20. Yes No   "My hobby is hang gliding."

---

you know. Be very careful about this; such information may strike the interviewer as gratuitous bragging. I remember one candidate describing his close friendship with a well-known broadcast luminary—how often they met, which social events they attended. I was trying to learn what the candidate could do for the employer; he seemed more interested in saying, "Look at who I know." A less objective interviewer might have seen him as a social climber, rather than the competent professional I found him to be. He got the job in spite of himself.

You need to use caution in talking about these topics:

- Your country club membership
- How much money you have
- Famous people in your family
- Living at a prestigious address
- Driving an expensive car
- Always traveling first class
- Graduating from a prestigious university

This is not to say you should never talk about these things; just be cautious when you mention them. Social standing can work for you or against you—and sometimes both.

I once participated in a series of interviews with a candidate who was being considered because he had graduated from the same top-name university as the CEO of the company. He mentioned his alma mater twice in an interview with line managers—most of whom had attended state colleges. They rated him intelligent, but not a good fit for the organization.

Confidential Information

Many organizations consider certain information confidential: trade secrets, proprietary technology, financial secrets, and so forth. Vendors and job candidates are sometimes asked to sign agreements not to disclose any such information they might acquire while visiting. If you seem too inquisitive, the interviewer may become suspicious of your intentions.

Suppose you are being interviewed for a government position that would give you access to protected information about nuclear weapons. If you ask questions, you must be careful to distinguish between public domain information and confidential information. The most practical guideline is not to ask for information that could not be published.

You should also use caution in asking about the organization's financial condition. You have a right to know whether the fiscal health of the organization might affect your long-term employment. On the other hand, insider information is off limits. This is often a judgment call, and asking the wrong question may not only raise suspicions but reveal your ignorance of the job you're applying for.

Key to "COMMENTS" on previous page: Yes on 2, 4, 7, 10, 13; no on the rest.

You should never expose confidential information regarding a current or former employer. To do so would be to break a confidence, which is unethical. The interviewer may take your willingness to share such information as a sign that you are not to be trusted, especially if you appear to be using it as a bargaining chip.

One other point: Suppose your interview is interrupted by a ringing telephone. Should you sit quietly until the interviewer is off the phone? No, etiquette suggests that you offer to leave the room to avoid overhearing a conversation the interviewer may consider private.

No Free Lunch

I read an article in which two businessmen told how they used lunch to find out what they wanted to know about a candidate's personal life: "When we take a female candidate to lunch, my partner and I begin talking with each other about our families—how old our kids are and what kinds of activities they participate in. After a while, the candidate wants to join the conversation. That's when we find out about her child care arrangements and whether she can really commit to doing the job." This way of thinking is commonplace. A casual lunch conversation that you may assume to be off the record may well be staged to discover personal things about you. There is no free lunch.

Another problem with mealtime interviews is that people have different, and often strong, preferences about food, table manners, and dinner conversation, and these personal attitudes often conflict with business rituals. An old friend of mine was once invited to dinner by a group of Asian prospects who were considering a business arrangement with his company. To show their great esteem, they served him a specially prepared soup made with fish eyeballs. He was aware that his reaction was critical to their evaluation of him. "I knew that the customs were different," he said. "I also knew what I was in for when I was invited to dinner. I did what was necessary to accept their hospitality."

Thoughts:

DANGER ZONES

Notwithstanding all the guidelines you may be given, you must use your best judgment and your sense of the interviewer's interest, values, and experiences in deciding which topics you may safely bring up in an interview. The following, however, are especially likely to get you into trouble. Be careful what you say about

- social causes, because the interviewer's opinions may be opposed to yours.

- politics, because the interviewer may vote differently.

- ethnic groups, because you may inadvertently insult the interviewer's relatives.

- age, because the interviewer may feel sensitive about getting older.

- disabilities, because you may be talking about the interviewer's spouse.

- gossip, because you may be talking about the interviewer's personal problems.

- alcohol, because the interviewer may have an alcoholic parent.

- offbeat hobbies, because the interviewer may think that you are strange.

- religion, because the interviewer may be an agnostic or atheist.

- money, because it may remind interviewers of their own problems.

- sports, because the interviewer may hate your team.

- name dropping, because the interviewer may not like your famous friend.

- name blasting, because the interviewer may be a friend of your enemy.

- health, because the interviewer may be battling health problems.

- schools, because the interviewer may have gone to a rival school.

I once had lunch with a client and one of his candidates, a friendly but professional person who had performed well in the interview. Upon being told we were going to Pappy and Jimmy's Lobster Shack, he grew excited and exclaimed that he had always wanted to eat at "Pappy's." At lunch, his professional demeanor gave way to an apparent obsession with the food. He attacked a bowl of clam chowder the way Sherman took Georgia, then finished his entrée in five minutes. Instead of using the time to sell his job skills, he rhapsodized about every morsel of food.

Later, in spite of my arguments that the candidate was well qualified, he was turned down. A free lunch should not be allowed to interfere with a promising career, but it can.

FROM THE HORSE'S MOUTH, AND MORE . . .

As you can see, many of the things that can get you into trouble can be identified because they are true of most people and most organizations. There are others, however, that you may be able to discover by networking. If you know fifty people you can ask about your prospective employer, one or two of them may be able to tell you something, or to steer you to someone else who knows about the organization or has worked there or knows somebody who . . . and so forth. In other words, using your contacts can keep you within five or six connections of millions of others, some of whom can help you anticipate the organization's norms and social expectations.

Of course, the most important single device that can determine whether you are seen as a cultivated, considerate candidate or a buffoonish boor is your mouth. Chapter 13 will explore how hoof-in-mouth disease can sink an otherwise attractive job seeker.

Thoughts:

Thoughts:

13

Watch
Your Mouth

In a one-hour selection interview, you will probably utter between five and ten thousand words; in a typical three-interview series, as many as thirty thousand. Now, here's something to give you pause: If you say 29,999 right words and one wrong one, you might as well have used your time standing on your head reciting the *Bhagavad-Gita*.

Words are the essence of communication—and miscommunication. The interview begins; you're nervous. You're not as eloquent as you were practicing at home alone, and you say something you don't mean. You leave out a key word and tell the interviewer exactly the opposite of what you intended . . . but you can do worse.

To emphasize a point, you use the word "damn." The interviewer is offended. He decides that, if you cannot express your ideas without using profanity, your communication skills must be inadequate. But you can do worse.

You hate the job you have now, and you mention how your crooked boss mismanaged the company, and how you intend to file a grievance and possibly a lawsuit. The interviewer decides you're a troublemaker with poor teamwork and conflict resolution skills . . . but you can do worse.

You're not sure you did well, and you'd like to get some feedback from the interviewer. But instead of simply asking him whether he found your responses helpful and suitable, you ask for suggestions on improving your interviewing skills. He infers that you're just using this interview as a practice session and have no intention of taking the job . . . but you can do worse.

Your personal life is not going well, and you can't help mentioning that you're in financial trouble because your ex-spouse maxed out your credit cards on a cross-country trip with a new lover. You hope the interviewer can sympathize. The interviewer does not. You can do worse . . . but it's hard to say how.

THE RAPPORT TRAP

A good interviewer can make it easy for you to say the wrong thing. By building an easy rapport, he can lead you to feel comfortable talking casually about sensitive matters, as if he were an old friend. And if he's a very good interviewer, he won't let a slip of the tongue hurt your chances badly if you show competence in job-related areas.

But not all interviewers are this dispassionate, and not all the self-defeating things you can say in the interview are mere slips of the tongue. Some candidates drop their guard completely and let their feelings override their common sense. I remember one candidate, a police officer, who spent much of the interview venting his disgust with his fellow officers, the chief, and the entire department. He had an uncontrollable need to talk about how he felt, rather than taking the opportunity to sell his skills. Instead of feeling confident in him, I felt sympathy for him—but not enough to recommend him for the job.

> **COACH'S TIP:** If you are of one race and your interviewer is of another, you may be tempted to volunteer the information that you are not biased. This is a mistake. Don't mention race at all. Avoid showing that you noticed a racial difference. Focus your attention on the job rather than on the ways that you differ from the interviewer.

Some candidates confuse the interviewer's friendliness for friendship. One candidate I interviewed kept talking about his upcoming divorce and arguments with his wife, things I didn't need to know and that had no relevance to the job. I began to realize that he wasn't just blowing off steam—he wanted me to sympathize with him. The realistic conclusion was that his work and his relationships with his fellow workers were likely to suffer because of his personal problems.

Never take advantage of the interviewer's willingness to listen by turning the interview into a counseling session. Control the impulse to talk about all the things that get your goat. Don't rant about liberals, right-wingers, environmentalists, dog lovers, vegetarians. Don't tell the interviewer lurid tales of organizational deceit, bad politics, misuse of authority, or harassment. If you insist on volunteering such information, remember this: it can work against you. You may be branded a complainer.

Always remember that the purpose of the interview is to provide information about your fitness for the job, and that irrelevant information not only takes away from the time you have to sell your skills but may well count against you. Stay focused on the job, and keep the interviewer's attention directed to the excellent work you can do for the organization.

THE RELIEF TRAP

When you come to the end of the interview, whether or not you think it's gone well, you'll have a tendency to let down your guard. The ordeal is nearly finished; the die is cast; for better or for worse, you feel there's not much you can do now to change the outcome.

And therein lies the trap. One interviewer told me that he had been interviewing a well-qualified engineer and was ready to offer him a job. Then he casually asked the engineer a simple question: "What would you do if you didn't get this job?" Without hesitation the engineer replied, "I'd sell my house, move to Colorado, and be a fishing guide."

Immediately the interviewer had doubts about the candidate's commitment to his career. The engineer was called in for more interviews but eventually went away without a job offer. He had let down his guard and expressed his until-then well-hidden desire to drop out. The momentary loss of control had cost him what was probably his best job prospect.

I don't mean to say that you shouldn't dream. Of course you should. Dreams are healthy, and when pursued purposefully, they often lead to a fulfilling life and career. But when you're being interviewed, remember that your goal is to get offered the position you're interviewing for. Think about each question before you open your mouth—especially those innocent little questions that come out of nowhere after you think you've bagged the offer.

WISH I HADN'T SAID THAT

I reviewed the notes I had taken over several hundred interviews to look for patterns of information. I was surprised to see how many candidates made comments that worked against them. To some extent, it's understandable; the interview can be an emotional experience, and it's easy to blurt out something you later wish you hadn't said.

But many candidates go into the interview not knowing that they shouldn't talk about the intimate details of their personal lives, rancorous disagreements with their former bosses, insecurity about their careers. Part of your preparation should be to review things that you might be inclined to say but shouldn't. That's why I'm using the rest of this chapter to show you what a lot of people said that they shouldn't have said.

I have paraphrased these quotes, changing details here and there to avoid any possible disclosure of the candidate's identify, but preserving the speaker's meaning. You may find some of them offensive, but I'm taking that risk to make you think: What might I say in all innocence that others might find offensive?

What We Have Here Is Failure to Communicate

"I disliked working with that overbearing, egotistical a__. Everything was always my fault. I ignored him and did the best job I could."

"My boss told me I was too nosy. I just turned and walked away. I pondered it a long time."

"We had a sales blitz. One person seemed to undermine it. I was upset. I said to myself, Why am I busting it? So I set the record straight: I handled it head on with my boss."

"There was one operator who stunk. I talked to him, told him he had to take a bath."

How I Managed Not to Manage

"I chewed his a__ out in front of all of them. I told him to get that look off his face or he could take a walk out the gate."

"He was noted for being a do-nothing. The work that had been required of him had been left undone. I stepped on his toes by doing all his jobs."

"I wander around 90 percent of the time in the office. I enjoy going to profit centers."

"I play fast-pitch softball. I'm a spikes-up type person, very aggressive."

"He seemed to think I was his key boy. . . . He gave me projects not related to my qualifications. I finally rebelled and said I can't do that."

"My nickname was Attila the Hun. I knew what my objectives were. . . . They respected me but I was disliked."

"Some of my people were found smoking dope. I couldn't attack all the problems at once. I should have been more aggressive."

"I liked him. He's a maverick; he's got the spirit of a mustang, not blind obedience. I cut him slack I wouldn't cut anybody else."

"Better to have made a decision and be wrong than get the damn thing through a bureaucracy."

"My ability to look at all adverse consequences to a decision bites me in the butt sometimes. . . . If I had done a couple hours extra work, I would have gotten more facts."

"My boss says I'm about as subtle as a freight train."

Got Them Work-Habit Blues

"I ruined $5,000 worth of equipment. I did exactly what my boss told me to do, even though I had reservations."

"What do you mean, get results?"

"My number one interest is big-screen football."

"I work in spurts."

"Planning of what? I don't have to organize a plan."

"Screw me once, shame on you; screw me twice, shame on me."

"My work cycle used to be pretty radical: a short cycle every two months, a low that lasts for a week."

"I expect a lot from my superiors."

"I nibble all day in the deli. I'm sneaky. They caught me twice."

I've Got a Secret

"The company is paranoid as hell. They hired and fired eight people in three months."

"I found out a reformed alcoholic I liked was on drugs. . . . One time my boss's brother shot him. I took the statements and explained to my boss. It resulted in an arbitration. The brother was fired. I stuck by the man he shot."

"When I was working in a squad car, we picked up the vice president of [Company Name], Inc. He was drunk, but instead of taking him to jail, we put him in a hotel room. We took his pants so he wouldn't leave the room."

"A lot of people don't like my boss. . . . A lady in another department had words with him and wanted to cry on my shoulder. I told her he just likes to agitate people."

Don't Hire Me, I Can't Cope

"I'm impatient. Incompetent people infuriate me. I get very upset, jump down people's throats. . . . I came down too strong on this one fellow, really reamed him out. I have a tendency to come on too strong."

"You can't make nobody know nothing."

SELF-ASSESSMENT: SAYING THE WRONG THING

Review the SHARE answers you developed back in chapter 7, then ask yourself the following questions aloud. You might tape-record them or practice in a small group with others who are preparing for interviews. Then evaluate each of your answers.

To what extent might your answer seem to indicate the following?

	1 Very Little	2 Little	3 Some	4 Great	5 Extreme
1. Willingness to use profanity	☐	☐	☐	☐	☐
2. Little self-understanding	☐	☐	☐	☐	☐
3. Autocratic management style	☐	☐	☐	☐	☐
4. Indecisiveness	☐	☐	☐	☐	☐
5. Tendency to make snap judgments	☐	☐	☐	☐	☐
6. Problems in coping	☐	☐	☐	☐	☐
7. Willingness to be deceptive	☐	☐	☐	☐	☐
8. Lack of integrity	☐	☐	☐	☐	☐
9. Overconfidence	☐	☐	☐	☐	☐
10. Uncooperativeness	☐	☐	☐	☐	☐
11. Lack of teamwork skills	☐	☐	☐	☐	☐
12. Failure to follow procedures	☐	☐	☐	☐	☐
13. Slow thinking	☐	☐	☐	☐	☐
14. Low work commitment	☐	☐	☐	☐	☐
15. Religious commitment or disbelief	☐	☐	☐	☐	☐

"I got so mad I had to walk off. My temper got me down."

"This one guy made me angry. . . . He had a lot on the ball, but had a habit of going to the office unnecessarily. . . . He thought I was dumb. One time I caught him. . . . I blew up. . . . I felt threatened."

"I thought he respected me. . . . He told me I was too immature. He thought my college education was a joke. I was crushed. . . . I was immature."

"I had a personality conflict with one of the vice presidents. I'm not sure why. . . . He drags me on the carpet for coming in fifteen minutes late three days in a row. During this time, the project manager had been out of the office for four days and was not reprimanded. . . . I kept working, but I wanted to punch his lights out."

"I'm very outspoken, and you know that can get you into trouble. . . . It's my temper. . . . I was short with my wife. She left home on me . . . sold her wedding ring for cash."

"As a police officer, I will not beat the hell out of someone for no reason at all."

More Than You Ever Wanted to Know, Period

"In a seminar, I met this guy. . . . I thought, Something's wrong here. . . . It turned out that he was trying to make love to my wife."

"My father and I were not friends."

"I used to have authority problems. . . . That's the reason I was in business for myself."

"I always hated my father as a child. . . . I later realized my mother was very ignorant, a small woman."

"I was a rebel. . . . In the military, I didn't like officers."

"I don't like to fail. . . . I don't have a lot of self-confidence."

"I require an extreme amount of stroking."

"I was losing perspective on my job. . . . I drank a lot. . . . The only thing that saved me was my people."

"I haven't been drunk in three years."

"I like the booze and parties pretty well . . . drinking heavily, chasing women."

"I was the class clown."

"I don't think I planned my life well enough. . . . I stumbled through a lot of things. . . . I should have finished school."

"My goal is to study my Bible more."

BENEFITING FROM THEIR MISTAKES

I asked several people to read these examples of interview self-destruction and give me their reactions. Here's some of what they told me:

"I was embarrassed for a person I don't even know."

"Some of these people didn't even have a clue!"

"I don't understand people who shoot their mouth off."

"I know the quotes are accurate, but I just can't believe that people would say things like this."

"People don't realize what they are saying."

The comments that seemed to create the most discussion were those that

- involved any form of profanity.

- reflected little self-understanding.

- indicated an autocratic management style.

- showed deception or a lack of integrity.

- depicted the individual as overconfident or lacking humility.

- made any reference to sex or religion.

Many of the people who wounded themselves with these comments got too comfortable and let down their guard. Another candidate, however, once said something that helped explain why so many people say things they shouldn't:

"When I was in the military, I would sit in the bar just to see what people talked about—you know, 'Loose lips sink ships.' I found that a moment of self-importance would cause other people to tell me things they shouldn't."

A good interviewer will make you comfortable, perhaps even self-important. You may be tempted to say what you shouldn't. This should raise alarms in your head. When rapport is high, think before you speak.

Before you say something on the edge of common sense, hesitate for a split second. Look at yourself from the others person's point of view. Watch yourself from afar, and hear yourself say what you are thinking of saying. How does it look? How does it sound? Is it a mistake? Is it a terrible mistake? Then don't say it. Curb your tongue. As American writer Elbert Green Hubbard once said, it is better to keep silent and be thought a fool than to speak and forever remove all doubt.

THE SHRINK WRAP

If you're like most of us, you'll come away from even a good interview with a vague feeling that you may have said the wrong thing once or twice. That's not something to get too concerned about. Nobody's perfect, and most interviewers discount the occasional slip of the tongue as meaningless.

So don't take it to heart if the interviewer asks you to meet the company psychologist. It's not a comment on your sanity, nor is it an illegal invasion of your privacy. It's the organization's way of evaluating whether you're likely to fit and work well within the organization, and it's a good sign that you're being seriously considered for the position. It's also the subject of the next chapter.

Meet
the Shrink

14

You've been through several interviews with the organization, you've presented yourself and your qualifications well, you've built good rapport, and watched your mouth. Things are looking up. You think you might get offered the job.

Then they send you to the corporate psychologist.

What did you do wrong? Was it something you said? Was wanting this job a sign of insanity? You picture yourself lying on a leather couch, spilling your childhood secrets, while a frowning Sigmund Freud, cigar ashes on his beard, rocks in his high-backed chair and scribbles in his note pad. You fear that some hideous flaw in your unconscious will leap from your mouth and Freud will arch his eyebrow and make a pronouncement about the depths of your mind.

Worse, you might not get the job.

THE CORPORATE PSYCHOLOGIST

Being interviewed by the corporate psychologist can be the most terrifying part of the screening process. It's not like a regular interview, where you have had a fair amount of experience.

With a psychologist, you may feel that your answers may convey more than you wanted to reveal. You may fear what will be discovered.

I am one of those corporate psychologists you worry about—more accurately referred to as industrial organizational, or IO, psychologists. We apply psychological principles to work issues involving individuals, groups, and organizations.

IO psychologists typically select specialties to work in. Many work in colleges and universities. Those in applied settings develop and validate tests, assess job candidates, conduct organizational surveys, coach executives, do team building and quality circles, and train workers on things like stress reduction and communication.

My special focus was on the selection interview. Over a twenty-year period I evaluated some 5,000 candidates for a wide variety of jobs using a combination of psychological tests and structured interviews. I met many uniquely qualified individuals who worried about what I would do, how I would do it, and how well they would measure up. Some probably did wonder about what dark secrets I would discover in the depths of their psyches. But that was not the intent of an assessment—the objective was to estimate the breadth and depth of the person's skills for doing effective work.

The IO psychologist typically sees the brightest, best-adjusted, best-educated, most motivated people. Her task may be to give feedback that helps the individual become an effective performer, to help management choose between exceptionally qualified candidates for a job, or to give a client tips on dealing with a difficult situation. Thus, you should consider it a compliment to be selected for assessment by or to get feedback from an IO psychologist.

Now I'm going to reveal what's behind all those mysterious assessments and tests, and you will see that it is not really so terrifying or dangerous after all. If you're prepared, and if you're the kind of person who will do well in the position to be filled, the psychological assessment will build even more confidence that you are the right person for the job.

THE SCIENCE OF ASSESSMENT

There is a big gap between the popular conception and reality of what an IO psychologist does. To begin, it is rare for an IO psychologist to come in contact with a client having major adjustment problems. IO psychologists almost always refer clients with emotional difficulties or family problems to clinical psychologists and counselors.

I have had people confess that they thought I could read their thoughts and discover their dark secrets. But this is all wrong. IO psychologists apply a science of assessment to make practical predictions and developmental plans regarding job performance. The competency model in chapter 5 is an example; it summarizes many of the things that an IO psychologist may try to measure in an assessment.

To ensure reliable results, evaluation methods are standardized by, for example, using a proven test instrument and reading questions in the same order for all job candidates. Individual rankings are based on results compiled from large numbers of tests.

You can verify the credentials of the person who will conduct your assessment. Use the Internet to find what schools she attended, what degrees she earned, and whether she has a license or state registration. Training and professional requirements vary greatly, but in general you should expect the assessment to be done by a person with a doctorate or a master's degree from an accredited university. Training should have included courses on job analysis, statistics, psychological testing, and supervised experience in selection and placement in the workplace. Ideally, you will find that the individual is active in professional organizations and published in the field.

WHY ARE ASSESSMENTS DONE?

It's natural to wonder why an organization would send you to see a psychologist as part of its screening process. There are many good reasons, ranging from life-or-death concerns to a natural interest in hiring well-adjusted individuals who will work together effectively. It's not because you're an outsider, either. Many organizations hire or retain psychologists to guide their employees' personal and career growth, prevent minor problems from becoming major ones, resolve conflicts, and help individuals and the organization function more smoothly.

Legal Requirements

Workers whose job performance could have public safety consequences are usually evaluated psychologically before being hired, and often at intervals during their careers. Many states require all law enforcement officers who carry a weapon to be assessed to determine whether they are legally sane. Federal regulations require complete psychological assessments for all nuclear power plant employees, including vendors who service equipment on site. Most airlines assess pilot candidates on such things as stability, decision making, and assertion. Then there is the question of due diligence in making hiring decisions—there may be a liability for an employer who does not screen out people who eventually harm co-workers.

Ultracompetitive Selection

When many well-qualified people apply for a few jobs that require extensive knowledge and intensive training, a psychological assessment may influence the final decision. Astronauts, for example, complete regular performance and psychological evaluations throughout their careers. Those who do not function at the highest levels psychologically may be sidelined or barred from the program. Airline pilots, police officers, military specialists, security officers, and intelligence officers fall into the same category.

Personnel Audits

Some organizations assess prospective and current employees as part of a personnel audit that will aid long-range succession planning. The audit becomes a continually updated measure of the talent and potential of managers and professional workers. It is kept separate from personnel files and used only by a select management group to help in making decisions about training, placement, and promotion.

Coaching Feedback

Assessment results are often used for executive coaching. Using information from surveys, interviews, and tests, the coach helps the executive identify one or more developmental targets and recommends actions to meet those objectives. Together they monitor what the executive does in particular situations, assess what was learned and what needs to be learned, and set new objectives for continuing improvement.

WHAT IT'S LIKE TO BE ASSESSED

You will probably be evaluated using one of two standard procedures: the individual assessment or the assessment center. In a typical individual assessment, a psychologist spends a day interviewing you and administering tests to evaluate your suitability for the job. The day begins with a brief meeting, followed by four to six hours of testing. At some point the psychologist interviews you, using a structured interview designed to elicit information about your work experience and competencies. Some assessors prefer not to test you but to rely on the interview alone. After the assessment, the psychologist reports to a contact within the organization, then follows up with a written report of the interview and test results.

An assessment center, unlike an individual assessment, typically brings together several candidates to complete exercises individually and as teams. Although designed by psychologists, an assessment center may be conducted by trained assessors, who observe candidates' behavior and compare notes on performance in group exercises or tasks designed to simulate work challenges. In a typical exercise, your behavior and suitability for the job may be evaluated based on competencies, such as those discussed in chapter 5, that the organization considers important.

Before the assessment begins, you will be told how the information will be used and who will have access to it. For promotion or selection, this usually means the organization only; your assessment will not be released to any other organization or person without your permission. In any case, the organization paying for the assessment generally treats your results as extremely confidential information.

If you are applying to go to work for the organization, you will probably not be offered access to the results. This privilege is usually reserved for internal promotion candidates or other internal assessments. However, if you end up getting the job, you may receive feedback to help you in your individual professional and personal development—not from a manager, but from a trained professional who can interpret your results.

STANDARD TECHNIQUES

Many different theories have been used in psychological assessments, and new ideas are continually being introduced into the field. In selecting people to fill jobs, however, IO psychologists generally use some combination of personality tests, structured interviews, and cognitive or ability tests. Typically, these approaches are standardized and often administered with the help of standard forms or computers.

Standard assessment techniques for employment do not include such things as dream analysis, word association, voice stress tests, handwriting analysis, or the use of colors for personality assessment. A few well-trained professionals in the past have used ink-blot tests, but that practice is so questionable that it is rare today.

Personality Assessment

Personality assessment can be broken into two broad categories—projective testing and standardized testing. Projective testing targets in-depth personality characteristics that may be traced to early childhood or traumatic experiences. It may be as simple as completing sentences read to you, or as complex as responding to ink blots or an ambiguous image. I think that standardized personality tests are better for workplace assessment than projective testing. They are typically based on years of research and provide evidence that they

DO I HAVE TO BE COMPLETELY HONEST ON THE PERSONALITY TESTS?

When you take a personality test, you will naturally wish to present yourself as positively as you can; you may be tempted to distort the truth. But test developers have constructed ways to compensate for efforts to make yourself look good. I won't say that it's impossible to fake a test, but I can say that it's not easy to outsmart a well-designed test. For example, consider the following question:

I would like to be

    a. a poet.

    b. an airline pilot.

    c. a restaurant owner.

When you read the question, you might say to yourself, "I'd really like to be a poet, but I don't want to sound like a wimp, so I'll say I'd rather own a restaurant." However, your guess about how each answer might be interpreted is probably wrong. "Poet" might score you high on creativity, whereas "restaurant owner" might get you a high mark on entrepreneurship, and "pilot" could mark you as adventurous. None of the interpretations involve any suggestions of weakness.

Some tests control the tendency for deception with forced-choice questions:

Circle the word in each pair that is most like you.

    1. irritating or hostile

    2. compulsive or impulsive

    3. thinking or feeling

Here the items are matched in terms of their desirability. Because you must respond to each question, you have to say some negative things about yourself. This makes it hard for you to distort your test results.

Personality measures often include honesty scales based on negatives that all people share:

Sometimes I am angry with people.

    a. True

    b. False

If you answer "True," you are admitting that you are like most people, because most people sometimes get angry with others. "False" may indicate that you're not very realistic about your possible negatives, or still worse, that you're trying to distort your test scores. With this approach, your overall profile can be statistically adjusted, based on your responses to these key questions, to counteract any attempt to skew your test results.

Here's my conclusion. Although you may influence your test results by answering dishonestly, the results will be unpredictable, and it is not likely that you can improve your assessment by doing so.

EXAMPLES OF PERSONALITY-BASED INTERVIEW QUESTIONS

"What critical event in your childhood has most influenced your managerial style?"

"Which of your parents are you most like, and how does your choice relate to your strengths and weaknesses at work?"

"Tell me what your biggest fears are on the job."

"When it comes to stress, how can you tell when you're reaching your breaking point?"

"Are you more tough-minded or tender-minded, and why?"

"Are you more spontaneous and intuitive, or more sequential and linear in problem solving?"

"Tell me what the word 'loyalty' means to you and explain how it relates to you as a person."

---

are valid. In order for either approach to be effective, the assessor must be highly trained, usually having a Ph.D. in psychology. A weekend seminar on a test is far from enough.

Sometimes standardized personality tests provide special formulas to make predictions for such traits as leadership, creativity, and stability. Formulas developed for specific jobs give the psychologist a statistical prediction of how well the candidate will perform in the job. Typically, these tests are available only to professionals trained in their use.

Structured Interviews

The interview is the most frequently used assessment technique. Basically, there are two varieties: structured and unstructured. An unstructured interview has no plan, no competencies to query or questions to ask. In contrast, a structured interview has a clear plan, with written questions organized under competencies.

When you see an IO psychologist, you can expect to take a structured interview. The psychologist will typically ask the questions without reading them verbatim. Most will take notes on what you say. It has been my preference to take notes in the form of direct quotes. If I miss information, I paraphrase what the candidate says. I record only the answers and avoid any interpretation.

A candidate once asked, after the interview, to see my notes. He was surprised when I agreed. But he was even more surprised to discover that I had written down only what he had said. As we discussed my approach, he realized that I didn't want to start interpreting his answers during the interview because that could bias the way that I proceeded with the assessment.

Behavior-based interviews. Behavior-based interviews are structured, with job-related questions organized under competencies. The interviewer usually does not ask all the questions, but rather selects the questions that seem appropriate for the current interview.

Behavior-based questions, as I explained in chapter 3, are singular, open-ended questions about past events. They are phrased to elicit information about how well you performed in a past work situation. For example:

"Tell me about a time when you worked hard to get results."

The answers are evaluated by comparing them with the competencies important for the job, using rating anchors. As a result, the competencies become a written standard for evaluating answers. Furthermore, the use of a standard procedure for comparison makes the behavior-based interviews reasonably objective, reliable, and valid for recommendations.

Biographical information blank. A biographical information blank is a close relative to a behavior-based interview, although it is clearly a questionnaire.

EXAMPLES OF BEHAVIOR-BASED INTERVIEW QUESTIONS

"Tell me about a time when you managed conflict effectively."

"Describe a situation in which you were able to effectively tell your boss some very bad news."

"Showcase your teamwork skills by describing a team problem that you were able to resolve."

"Describe an incident in which you failed to communicate as effectively as you could have."

"Give me an example of a way that you were able to organize yourself on your last job."

"Describe a mistake you made in the last six months, tell me what you learned from it, then give me an example of how you used your learning."

"Can you think of a time when you used common sense to justify breaking an important rule at work?"

"When have you been most guilty of being lazy on the job?"

Originally patterned after an application blank, it is a life-history questionnaire designed to predict, with a quantitative score, your future job performance based on how your background compares with that of previous successful employees—your education, job longevity, whether you grew up on a farm, and so forth. This approach, elaborated over many years, has emerged as a highly effective selection instrument for specific jobs.

A typical biographical information blank might include fifty or more questions like these:

1. What number best reflects the size of the town you lived in before you were 12?
   a. Under 5,000
   b. Between 5,001 and 25,000
   c. Between 25,001 and 100,000
   d. Between 100,001 and 1,000,000
   e. Over 1,000,000

2. At what age did you first earn money?
   a. Under 5
   b. Between 5 and 8
   c. Between 9 and 12
   d. Between 13 and 16
   e. Between 17 and 20
   f. Over 20

3. What best describes the level of encouragement you received about your education before you were 20 years old?
   a. Attend high school
   b. Graduate from high school
   c. Attend vocational school
   d. Attend college
   e. Graduate from college
   f. Earn a master's degree or a doctorate

Situational questions. In a situational interview, you are asked hypothetical job-related questions that involve a "what if" dilemma requiring you to choose a course of action. This approach measures your intentions, rather than your

EXAMPLES OF SITUATIONAL INTERVIEW QUESTIONS

"You just came out of management training, where you learned how critical it is to follow procedures in your job, but now you are assigned to a manager who likes to do things intuitively. What would you do if your manager gave you a direct order that was inconsistent with procedures?"

"You're assigned to the third shift. Your spouse and children are sick with colds, and you're starting to feel symptoms. Your shift starts in three hours. What would you do?"

past actions. It is nevertheless behavior-based, because it uses your current behavior—that is, your verbal behavior in the interview—as the basis for prediction. It is also job related, because each question concerns actions you would take in a hypothetical work situation.

Cognitive-Based Assessment

Cognitive assessment is the measurement of intelligence. Employers who use this approach base predictions about your job performance on your skills in solving problems involving such things as vocabulary, comprehension, mathematics, spatial visualization, and memory.

A typical cognitive assessment procedure is a standardized problem-solving test on which you must answer as many questions as you can, either within a specified time or at your own pace. If you have a physical disability that would put you at a disadvantage on a timed test, tell the administrator; an untimed test can usually be substituted.

EXAMPLES OF COGNITIVE-BASED INTERVIEW QUESTIONS

1. How many miles is it from the earth to the moon?

2. Name the four main food groups.

3. What does "façade" mean?

4. What is the square root of eighty-one?

5. What is the relationship between torque and inertia?

6. Explain what is meant by H_2O.

7. How many grains of sand would there be in a one-gallon container?

SHOULD I GUESS ON PROBLEM-SOLVING TESTS?

When taking ability tests you will probably be asked to solve verbal problems, which involve vocabulary and logical reasoning, and numerical problems in basic arithmetic and number sequences. If you'd like a preview of the kinds of questions you'll be asked to solve, pick up one of the many books on preparing for college entrance exams.

On some tests you are penalized for wrong answers; on others you are not. The instructions should tell you whether it's in your favor to try to guess answers you are unsure of. If necessary, ask the test administrator. If there's no penalty for wrong answers, respond with your best guess. If wrong answers count against you, skip the ones you aren't reasonably sure of.

For years stories have made the rounds that such tests have a secret pattern of correct responses—for example, that on every fourth question "a" is the right answer. I cannot imagine why any candidate would believe that test developers would build in such a pattern as a cue to help the test taker beat the system. Actually, they go to great lengths to avoid doing so; anyone who designed beatable tests would soon be found out and professionally discredited.

It is very important to understand and follow the instructions exactly. Some of the questions will be easy for you, but you probably won't be able to answer all of them correctly, because these tests are designed to measure up to a very high level of problem solving abilities. Don't feel bad if you can't answer all the questions; not many people can.

If you are given a computer-based cognitive test, the display will give you instructions, present questions, time your responses, and compile the results. This ensures that the test is administered and scored the same for all candidates.

THE NEXT STAGE

The interviews and testing are over. Now the waiting begins. You're entering a stage in your search when your fate rests largely in the hands of others.

What do you do? Just sit and wait? What if you are told that the job won't be filled? What if you have to wait for weeks for the offer to come through? What if someone else gets your job?

Well, let's be smart about this. Don't shut down your search because you expect to get an offer. This is the time to develop your next interview targets and to take more interviews. Keep looking until you get a firm offer. Keep different alternatives, different paths, in front of you.

Thoughts:

GET READY FOR THE NEXT CHALLENGE

It's not an uncommon experience to feel that an interview has gone badly, only to discover later that everything was fine. The period immediately after the interview is often a time when your tension and anxiety rise and your fears of unemployment resurface. You've done all you can do, and now your fate is in the hands of others.

This may be the hardest part of the whole process, especially for people who are disposed to action and feel edgy when events are out of their control. But, as you will see, there is still much you can do to move yourself in the right direction. And there is much you need to do to keep your spirits up, your opportunities growing, and your priorities straight.

The next two chapters are about using your post-interview time constructively. Chapter 15 will show you how you are evaluated for the position, and how you can help your chances by anticipating some of the things your prospective employers will talk about. Chapter 16 offers philosophical advice on what to do if you're not offered the job, and—perhaps equally important—what to do if you're offered the job but have second thoughts about taking it.

15

BEHIND CLOSED DOORS

You've filled out all the forms, taken all the tests, talked with everyone you can get in touch with. You feel like you've been interviewed by everyone in the organization. Now what do you do?

In many ways, this is the toughest part of the process. You've done all you can—or so it seems—and now your fate rests in the hands of people who are talking about you behind your back. You wait, and you worry. What's happening behind those doors?

HOW DECISIONS GET MADE

As a facilitator in a personal growth laboratory designed to help participants improve their communication skills, I regularly led an exercise called the "fishbowl." Three people sat in a circle and discussed a problem they all faced at work. A second group of three silently watched the three "fish" and took notes on how effectively they communicated. After fifteen minutes, the observers and the fish swapped positions. The observers spent their time in the fishbowl talking about how the three

BE NUMBER THREE

I've heard many people say your chances are best if you're the third candidate interviewed. I never put much stock in this idea until I began regularly teaching interviewing to interviewers. Many of them said they liked to have three candidates to interview: one was a no, another a maybe, and the third a hire.

Still I remained skeptical. I had interviewed as many as six candidates in one day without finding a single one that I would hire. On the other hand, sometimes I recommended the first person I interviewed. Why? Because I always compared the candidates' responses to job-related selection criteria.

Many interviewers don't know exactly what they are looking for. Instead, they compare candidates with one another. Three seems to be the ideal number for these comparisons; two is not enough, and four seems like extra work.

Most interviewers need time to warm up. With candidate one, they're having their first cup of coffee and limbering up their technique. Candidate number two affords additional practice and builds the interviewer's confidence. With the third candidate, the interviewer is awake, relaxed, attentive, comfortable, and eager to make a decision.

So you may have a slight advantage if you're the third candidate of the day. This is far from being an absolute; many other factors influence a competent interviewer's discussion. It's also an area where you have little control. You can't ask the interviewer to let you be candidate number three. But if you're asked which time would be most convenient—8:00, 9:30, or 11:00—pick eleven.

The true advantage comes from being aware that many interviewers need time to warm up. A greater advantage comes when your responses to questions match the selection criteria and are better than those of your competitors.

---

people they had observed could communicate better. The people who were being discussed had to sit outside the bowl and hear how they were perceived by the observers. Fifteen minutes later they were back in the fishbowl, describing what they heard and saw the others do when they communicated. After two rounds, everyone participated in an open discussion; then all six participants dealt with the original work problem.

I have often thought of the fishbowl exercise while helping an interview team decide on a candidate. I always wondered what the candidate might say after watching this process. At times I would have been proud to have the candidate listen. In other cases, the candidate would surely have been shocked to see how poorly some interviewers used the information gained in the interview.

In my work with interview teams, I got to see for myself how unfair subjective impressions can be. In one team discussion of several candidates, one interviewer wanted to hire a candidate because he was a "good Joe" who would fit in well with the existing work team. I considered another candidate better qualified; to hire the "good Joe" because of one interviewer's subjective reaction would have been unfair to the other candidate. When I asked him for an interview example that would support his recommendation, his face got red, he raised his voice, and he shook his finger at me.

After this outburst, the selection team reviewed the qualifications of all candidates more objectively. Looking back on the experience, I like to think I was protecting a person from an arbitrary decision. But you may not be so lucky; there may be no one on the interview team who will argue for an objective decision.

Although your most active part in the process is over, you don't have to feel helpless. There's a lot you can do after the interview, while your potential employers are deliberating your fate, to improve your chances of getting a job offer. You can use the time constructively to increase your chances of getting a good job—whether this one or another. You can develop additional knowledge skills and abilities that will give you an edge over other qualified job candidates. And

COMMENTS MADE ABOUT CANDIDATES

In the meeting that follows your interview, interviewers usually have different things to say about your performance. Here are some of the things I've heard. The sample comments below suggest that you should use a positive-impression strategy with the subjective interviewer and an information strategy with the objective interviewer.

"She didn't appear to be career oriented."

"He's too good-looking to work here. He'll distract the whole staff."

"It would seem strange with her driving the pumper truck."

"His belt didn't match his shoes."

"The customers won't respect her."

"He looks like an old hippie."

"I just don't feel she'll fit in with the team."

"He needs to lose about eighty pounds."

In short, you must generate as many positives as possible to counteract subjective comments.

you can debrief yourself—that is, review your performance in the interviews, tests, and other parts of the process—to see what you could do better next time.

CONSTRUCTIVE WAITING

The conventional wisdom says to write a follow-up letter after the interview to your primary contact reaffirming your interest in the job—and this time, the conventional wisdom is right. Now that you've been through the process, you know more about the organization than before. From the questions they asked, you know their interests, their concerns, their expectations. You know more about the job. Now you can follow through by offering more information about your experience, skills, and abilities that can help them see you as the best candidate to fill the position.

It's also a good idea to monitor your progress through information contacts with your advocate—or, if you haven't developed an advocate, the contact who arranged for your interview. Do so cautiously; sometimes the line between showing interest and appearing too eager is next to invisible. Remember that the interviewer has many other responsibilities, so don't make a pest of yourself.

Most candidates tend to be either optimistic or pessimistic about their chances of getting the job. Until you hear one way or the other, don't assume anything. One interviewer told me of a candidate with whom he had had great rapport and who had done very well in the interview. Unaware that he was competing with another highly qualified person and assuming that he would get the offer, the candidate quit his job to take some time off before starting the new job. He was shocked to discover that the position had gone to the other candidate; the interviewer was shocked that the candidate had made such an unwarranted assumption.

Sometimes you just don't know what to think. Maybe you're waiting to hear about your dream job, the kind of work you've spent years looking for and for which you think you'd be perfect. Because your hopes are so high, you find it hard to function normally. You wait for the phone to ring; you lose sleep; you worry. All this anxiety is wasted energy. If you get the job, you've worried unnecessarily, and if you don't, you've wasted time you could have spent productively.

The best way to spend your time after an interview is to keep looking for opportunities. This has many potential benefits:

- You turn your anxiety into productive energy.

- You will not appear overeager.

- You develop contacts to use if the job doesn't come through.

- You may find an even better job opportunity.

- You put yourself in a better negotiating position.

TIEBREAKERS

Sooner or later the question arises, "What if it's between me and another candidate with similar qualifications?" How do interviewers make decisions with candidates who are equal? They use tiebreakers.

Some tiebreakers are best described as "value added"—characteristics, skills, or experiences that go beyond job requirements but offer added value to the

---

KEEP LOOKING!

One of my friends recently went through a particularly demanding job search. Here is what he told me:

"I was very aware that my job might be eliminated. I had a high salary, and my division was being acquired by a larger company whose existing staff could easily assume my job responsibilities. Nevertheless, I still felt a sting of anxiety when I was told I would be outplaced.

"There were special problems in my situation; the economy was bad, and for family reasons I felt I couldn't move. I also simply couldn't stand being out of work. I hadn't been out of a job since I was thirteen. I decided I wasn't going to be one of those guys who were still looking for a job three years after being outplaced. I'd go for the best job I could get, but I knew I'd be working, even if I had to drive a truck like I did in my early twenties.

"One of my first interviews was for my dream job—it was actually an advance over my last job. But while I was waiting for an offer, I continued to use my time to get other interviews. Although I felt confident about getting the job, I wanted to keep my options open. I worked twelve hours a day looking for new opportunities.

"I didn't get my dream job. But I wasn't dead in the water when I got the news. I used my momentum to network with venture capitalists. I got a three-month consulting job, which put me in line to replace a person who would retire in six months. I kept looking for interviews while I was consulting. But at the end of the consulting job I got an offer to stay full time.

"Paul, my advice to your readers is never stop looking while waiting for a job offer. It paid off for me. Some of the people who lost their jobs when I did aren't working yet."

organization. When you're competing for a job, value-added skills may tip the scales for the candidate with more to offer. Other tiebreakers are more situational, such as how close you live to the job. Still others may simply reflect interviewer preferences—some of which may have merit, others of which may be questionable.

Breadth of skills. Candidates with a broad range of skills beyond job qualifications seem to have an advantage when decisions are close. For example, the CPA who also has a real estate license, the programmer who knows telephonics, the salesperson who can speak German—these candidates may be more attractive to the organization.

Geography. Where you live can work for you or against you, depending on the location of the job. The most obvious consideration for the employer is to avoid paying your moving costs. Of less significance is the distance you would have to commute. A candidate with a fifteen-minute commute may be more desirable than one with a ninety-minute commute. Your ability to access a major airport can be important if you are being considered for a job that requires travel.

The previous job holder. If the last person failed in the job, any similarity between that person and you may work against you. The interviewer doesn't want to make the same mistake twice. Suppose you do well in the interview, but it turns out that you graduated from the same college as the last holder of the job. If it comes down to you and another person who is equally qualified, the organization, fearing that you will fail just like your predecessor, may hire your competitor. Unfortunately, there's not much you can do about this.

Diversity. Organizations that recognize the financial advantages of competing in diverse markets tend to place a high value on a diverse workforce. Being a member of any protected category—gender, race, color, religion, national origin, age, or disability—may give you the advantage if there is a close call between you and another candidate.

Employment fees. Some organizations place more confidence in candidates who have been screened by a search firm or a placement organization, and consider the costs of finding the right people minor when weighed against their potential productivity. Other organizations prefer to do their own recruiting. The only way to predict whether a recruiting firm will help or hurt your job chances is to know how the employers feel about paying others to screen their candidates.

DON'T GET A LAWYER, GET A JOB

Now that you're past the interview and waiting for your potential employer to make a decision, you may think back and remember one or two questions that seem discriminatory to you. You may even have thought them illegal at the time but refrained from challenging the interviewer. If so, you probably made a wise decision, one that will redound to your advantage.

You're in a good position. You have several possible courses of action: If you're offered the job, you can

- accept the offer and—on the assumption that the illegal questions represent only the interviewer's bias, not the organization's—go to work.

- decline the offer because you do not wish to work for an organization with such obvious bias against you.

On the other hand, if you do not get the offer, you can

- ask the company to reconsider because you feel the selection process was biased.

- bring legal action against the company for its discriminatory hiring practices.

- chalk it up to experience and be better prepared to respond the next time you feel you are subjected to biased questioning.

If you choose to bring legal action, you may have a good case, one that may eventually bring you a favorable settlement. Keep in mind, however, that you must balance your chances of winning against a large expenditure of money, aggravation, and especially time—hours, days, and months that might be used more productively in a career at another organization that will treat you more fairly.

Athletic skills. If the organization has sports activities, your athletic experience may figure in your chances of getting hired. One interviewer I heard of, hoping to win the league championship, hired a former college baseball player over other, more qualified, candidates as a ringer on his company team.

Branch of military service. It's not unusual for former military people to prefer candidates who have served in the military—especially their own branch of the service. If you were a marine and the interviewer was a marine, you have the inside track over an equally qualified ex-army candidate. An applicant with equivalent skills developed through civilian training may be shut out altogether.

A SELF-INTERVIEW

After you've gone through an interview, ask yourself the following questions in order to learn from your experience.

Before the interview—did I

- confirm my interview in writing or telephone?
- ask to pick up a job description?
- ask associates about the organization's culture?
- thank my advocate or contacts who helped me get the interview?
- review published company information?
- prepare my clothing ahead of time?
- arrive on time?
- check my grooming immediately before the interview?

Rapport building—did I

- thank the interviewer for the interview?
- smile?
- avoid nervous gestures?
- correctly use the interviewer's name?

Startup questions—did I

- get a descriptive question, like "What can you do for us?" If so, did I respond with a skill-based answer?

Hobbies. Like other tiebreakers, your hobbies can work for you or against you. Some, like hang gliding or collecting guns, may strike the interviewer as frivolous, expensive, strange, or dangerous. More helpful are hobbies linked with your career; an electrical engineer whose hobby is building computers is likely to gain tiebreaker points. Some employers want all your spare energy, and some candidates cater to that preference; as one executive told me, "Job first, family second. There's nothing left for hobbies."

Team experience. It used to be a factor in your favor if you played team sports; employers considered this evidence that you could work well with others. Team experience faded as a selection factor during the sixties and seventies but has made a comeback because of the current emphasis on quality work teams. If

- get a work-history question, like "Review your education and career for me"? If so, did I respond with an emphasis on the skills I learned and the achievements they were associated with?

Interviewer style:
- What did I do to adapt to this interviewer's style?
- What types of skill-benefit statements did this interviewer seem most interested in?
- What mistakes did I make with the interviewer's style?
- What was the best answer that I gave in this interview?
- Did I seem natural in using my SHARE answers?
- What was a "killer" question that I had? How did I answer it? How do I evaluate my response?

Comments, manners:
- What did I say that may work against me in getting the offer?
- Did I say or do anything that might be inconsistent with this organization's culture?

Wrap-up:
- Did I get the interviewer's card?
- Did I ask about the next step in the process?
- Did I contact my advocate for feedback on the interview?

---

you have had productive experiences in work teams, bring them out in the interview. If you haven't, indicate that you are adaptable to the needs of co-workers and customers.

DEBRIEFING YOURSELF

If you're the type of individual who learns quickly from experience, you'll recognize the interview as a very important and valuable learning experience. Now you have a little time to pause and reflect. What type of interview was it? Did you answer the questions as effectively as you could have? If you had it to do over, what would you do differently?

What you learn from the interview can be helpful the next time you interview with another organization. Think of it as a data bank that you can draw on for your next project—getting a good job. But it can also pay dividends right away. In a close situation, when you and another candidate are similarly qualified and the company is not yet ready to decide, you may be called back for another interview. If you've thought about your last interview, you can give yourself an edge by adapting your approach.

When the interviewers meet behind closed doors to discuss your interview performance, their decision will depend largely on whether their approach to the selection process is basically objective or subjective. Gut-feel and conversational interviewers will tend to focus on one or two of your responses—those they reacted to most strongly. With such interviewers, especially the gut-feel interviewer, you must be careful to avoid making the one comment that might kill your chances. Think back on the interview: Did the interviewer react strongly to anything you said? Did the rapport cool noticeably? Can you identify any factor that changed the feel of the interview? If you can, avoid that subject in any follow-up interview and in future job interviews.

Interviewers who use a structured approach, such as behavior-based interviewers, will compile and score your answers using standard methods before they discuss your interview performance. They are much less likely to let one or two of your responses keep you from getting the job.

THE DOORS SWING OPEN

After the organization has made its decision whether or not to hire you, you are faced with one further decision of your own: Will you accept their offer? Remember, it's a two-way street, and after experiencing a taste of your potential employer in this selection process, whether you are rejected or not, you may discover that other alternatives are not that bad—as we will discuss in the final chapter.

Thoughts:

16

THE ROAD NOT TAKEN

In the summer after my junior year in college, I had a job at the Shelby County Penal Farm. All summer I took prisoners out to cut grass along country roads. One of them—a man the other prisoners called "Pigpen" because of his sloppy habits—was an expert in surviving prison life. I learned one of my most important life lessons from him, for Pigpen was very clever. He knew how to find work and make money, even in prison.

One day I saw Pigpen making what appeared to be a set of reins. I watched, puzzled. He attached them to the steering wheel of his mowing tractor. Then he started the tractor, put it in gear, lowered the blade and began walking after it, tugging on the reins to guide it. "Just like plowing with a mule!" he said.

He had figured out a way to moonlight. While his tractor cut grass, Pigpen would walk behind it and collect bottles, worth a few cents each in deposits. At the end of the day he would have ten dollars' worth of bottles. Day after day Pigpen's net worth grew. Among the prisoners, Pigpen was upper middle class.

Pigpen was an entrepreneur, an innovator, a go-getter. Although he didn't know it, he was an inspiration for me. Like any young person, I worried about not having enough money. Pigpen showed me my fears were groundless. If Pigpen could make a buck in prison, surely I could do as well on the outside, with an education and unlimited opportunity.

Since then, I have often thought of Pigpen. When I failed to get something I wanted, I would remember how Pigpen would live by his wits and cheerfully make do with what was at hand. It didn't take much money to make him happy. Surely I could do as well. No need to get upset; my skills would meet my basic needs. My disappointments were over things I wanted, not things I needed.

A person in my training class was telling us how his last job had evaporated because his boss didn't like him. As he was describing his unhappiness in that job and how he felt he had been persecuted, suddenly something occurred to him. "You know," he said, "after I lost my job, none of the really important things changed. My health was good, my family was okay, and we paid our bills. The experience made me stay in touch with what was really important to me."

This is Pigpen's lesson to us all. As the Rolling Stones remind us, you can't always get what you want, but you may just get what you need. Sure, it's nice to be offered the job, to feel wanted—but fate may give you something you need instead. Keep this in mind when the option is yours. Your joy at being accepted may keep you from seeing that you'd be better off doing something else.

In many years of listening to people review their careers, I have found a common thread. When they hired on for meaningful work, they usually enjoyed their jobs and had good relationships with the people they worked with. Then they took jobs for other reasons—location, money, status—they often ended up disliking their work and most of their co-workers.

ALTERNATIVE WORKSTYLES

When you are offered the job you so diligently sought, remember this: the final decision is yours. Do you really want to do the work? Are you well suited for it? Listen to your feelings. It may be a plum job with lots of money and prestige, but will you be happy? Just because you liked this kind of work in your last company doesn't mean that you'll like it in this one, where they do things differently and you don't know the people. In the ever changing workplace, the job you used to have probably doesn't exist anymore.

People still want meaningful work, but a career ladder seems to be a vanishing dream, tossed out with the excess layers of management that corporations are slicing away. Self-managed work teams and fewer supervisors are probably just around the corner for you, if you're not already there.

HOW BAD CAN AN INTERVIEW BE?

Here's a story told to me by a job candidate who, after an apparently successful interview outcome, decided not to take the job.

"The interviewer leaned back in his chair, put his feet on the desk, and said, 'Tell me about yourself.' Right away, I felt I was wasting my time."

"I began telling him about myself, but soon found myself listening to his life history—where he went to school, his love of football, why he chose a career in sales, on and on through the first ten minutes of the interview. I guess he thought that by using this approach he was building rapport with me. Actually, he just seemed self-absorbed."

"When he was able to tear his attention away from himself, he asked me to describe my strong point. I told him I was organized. Then he asked about my weakest trait. I said that people told me I spent too much time at work. He seemed pleased with my weakness, even though my answer was obviously self-serving."

"He asked me about my job plans. As I was describing my career goals, his expression took on a wariness that made me think, This guy doesn't want anyone around who could get his job. I realized I had made a mistake: I had seemed too ambitious. Suddenly I was afraid I had killed my prospects.

"Toward the end, he began talking about his wife and family. I had the feeling he was trying to get me to talk about my personal life—but instead of revealing my private life, I asked him questions about his experiences at work. This seemed to make him like me more. He appeared not to realize I was interviewing him."

"Later they offered me the job. I turned it down. Who wants to work with someone so self-centered?"

On the other hand, you may not want to do the kind of work you used to do. Like many others, you may prefer to redesign your work style to better accommodate your personal needs. Many bold spirits now go looking not for a job but for work that is spiritually fulfilling: "Life's too short to put up with what I used to have to do." See if you can identify with any of the following people.

URBAN SURVIVAL

Until about twenty years ago, an acquaintance of mine worked for a major corporation. After deciding that he couldn't stand the politics and stress of his job, he got a position in a government agency, but was invited to leave after two years. The recognition dawned on him that work in the traditional sense of the word was just not for him. He became what I call an urban survivalist, living off his ingenuity.

A college-educated man of average intelligence, more relaxed than driven, he was good with his hands, and could live happily on next to nothing. He grew a garden behind his house to supplement his grocery shopping. He didn't have to dress for work. He was out of debt. With time on his hands, he used some of his savings to divide his house into an apartment that earned him extra cash.

He started doing odd jobs and carpentry. Over time he saved enough money to buy a second property, which he made into two apartments that increased his cash flow. He continued to do odd jobs and looked for deals to make extra money.

A JOB DECISION INTERVIEW

The following structured self-interview is built around what I have found to be key factors in making an effective job decision. Many of these are issues that job candidates have raised when discussing mistakes they made in their careers, jobs they have taken when they shouldn't have, jobs they have turned down that would have been good for them. Ask yourself these questions, or have a friend interview you. Write down your answers and think about them. It will help you determine whether the job you want truly fits your needs.

Job Search

- How effective and committed have you been in your job search? Are you pursuing your career goals systematically and with perseverance?

- Have you contacted enough organizations to attain a good understanding of the value of your skills in the marketplace?

- Have you prepared well for your interviews? Has a lack of preparation limited your ability to get job offers?

- Have you been open to opportunities in organizations that do not have a well-known image?

Job Situation

- Is the work to be done in a desirable location?

- Are you satisfied with the compensation and benefits of the job?

- Will this job situation be consistent with your family's needs?

Today this man has well over a million dollars in paid-for real estate and a healthy cash flow. He has been to Europe more times than I have and has more friends than a politician. Now he's talking about buying a shrimp boat and working and living on it for a while.

Look at him today and you see a person who is both personally and financially successful. And this happened because he chose never again to hold a traditional job. Just as farmers have been able to live on their land with a modest income, he has been able to live off of his apartments as an urban survivalist. He is happy.

Family First

I first met Thomas at a friend's party. He held a senior management position and had a bright future. He was smart, good looking, and capable. He was also

- Does this organization have a positive reputation? Will you feel proud telling people where you work?

- Does this organization have products that are consistent with your beliefs? Do the products promote health, safety, and a clean environment?

- Does this organization deal with people on their merits, rather than discriminating against them based on gender, race, color, national origin, religion, age, or disability?

Job Context

- Will the culture of the organization fit your working style?

- Does the organization have the fiscal ability and determination to protect your job? If not, are you willing to risk your career for the possible rewards?

- Does this organization encourage you to express your opinions and participate in decision making, or is it autocratic, deciding issues from the top down?

Job Content

- What aspects of the job (travel, entertainment, ambiguity, ethics) might cause you to become dissatisfied with it?

- Does this job fit your long-term career goals?

- Will this job let you meet your own standards for honesty and integrity?

facing the prospect of a move to Minneapolis because his employer closed out the local offices and required all senior management to work out of the corporate offices. Rather than move, Thomas accepted outplacement.

When I had the chance to talk with him later, he told me his reasons for staying put. He and his family loved their home; his children were doing well in school; he didn't feel that money was everything. I was surprised—I had never perceived him as a family-first man. But my perceptions were wrong. Thomas put his family above his career.

Thomas was very skilled at networking. He quickly lined up interviews, some with out-of-town employers who would let him live wherever he chose. Then came the dream job. It was in Chicago, but it was so attractive that Thomas had to consider it. He and his family looked at condos in the city. He imagined what it would be like going to work every day in a limousine.

But Thomas turned down the job. He started a consulting company and now has several people working with him. He is financially successful. His family is happy. He is doing what he wants to do. When the job offers failed to match up with his wants, Thomas was able to say no.

Learn Your Way Out

Over the years I've had long-term consulting projects that enabled me to get to know the people in an organization very well. In one organization there was an extremely able woman—professional, college educated, and certified in her field. Her manager told me that she was going through a horrible divorce and facing several financial problems. Her personal problems didn't affect her work, but they did make her question what she was going to do with her life.

This woman attended a time-management class I was teaching, in which one of the assignments was to set short-term and long-term goals. She said that her goal was to get a doctorate in English within six years. She wanted to do business writing and was especially interested in international business. Many of her goals were very specific: the amount of money she would be making in ten years, the car and home she would own.

Soon thereafter, she enrolled in a graduate program. Offered an assistantship and a grant, she quit her job and earned her degree quickly. She has since returned to the organization in an entirely new role and has achieved her professional goals. She had taken advantage of a personal disaster to move in an entirely new direction; education was both her escape and her road to higher goals.

Absolute Commitment

I have not been yelled at by many clients, but here's a story about a man who did just that. He was so committed to the idea of owning his own business that he wouldn't listen to reason. He had little cash and no experience in his chosen line of business. I told him three times, as tactfully as I could, that the odds were very much against him. That's why he yelled at me. As it turned out, he was right and I was wrong. His blind commitment to his goal paid off.

Before you think I am encouraging you to set unrealistic goals, let me tell you that this man was a very driven individual with a strong intellect. He had many useful personal assets: his family was behind him 100 percent, and he had more contacts than any two people. However, his biggest asset was his determination to own his own business.

By now you can guess how the story unfolds. He found a good business for sale and got on good terms with the owner, who wanted to retire. He financed his startup with money from his retirement plan and a second mortgage on his home. He learned the business quickly and made it grow, and grow, and grow. I'm sure he's quite wealthy by now.

When he yelled at me, I thought he was out of control. I was wrong. He was and is very much in control of himself—both in work and in life. His high standards sent him in quest of work that he liked instead of just another job. This kind of commitment can be a lesson for us all.

The Death Dream

A close friend of mine quit his job in a major corporation after having what he called a "death dream":

> I woke up in the middle of the night in a cold sweat. I had dreamed that I was an old man, sitting at the same desk in the same office that I have now. My boss walked in, but he was now very old, too. He started his usual high-pressure game and even in my dream my stomach knotted up just like it does now at work.
>
> I was relieved that it was just a dream. But the horrible feeling lingered until I realized that the dream was a warning about something very real that was happening to me. I was dying a slow death in my job. The only reason I went to work was to get money. The only friends I had at work were political communication channels. My enemies were ready to misconstrue anything I said and raise doubts about anything I did.
>
> My death dream told me that I had to leave my well-paid job in a highly respected organization. My greatest career risk was staying, not going.

My friend resigned on the day that he had fifteen years of tenure in the organization, the cutoff point for his long-term retirement benefits. He called his boss from a public phone in the Denver airport, explained that he was planning to leave, and offered to make the transition as painless as possible. His boss appreciated the gesture but suggested they could fill the job internally with no problems.

The last time I spoke with this person he was positive that he had done the right thing. He has a new job in a new industry and says he's never been happier.

Each of these stories shows how you can use your innate wisdom and courage to find meaningful work. In each case the individual pursued a goal, stated or unstated, that combined personal desires with work opportunities—a work search, not a job search.

BUILDING BRIDGES BEHIND YOU

Here is some of the best advice I ever got: "Don't burn any bridges behind you. If things don't work out, you may have to work for that person again."

When you accept a job, remember everyone you talked with along the way. If you don't accept it, remember the people who took the time to assess your skills and recruit you for the position. And when you are rejected, say thank you for your time. Each of the people you talked with may be a gateway for new opportunities later on. At a minimum, keep business cards and phone lists handy for future job searches.

You may stay in touch with an interviewer with whom you've established good rapport. People I interviewed years ago call now and then just to stay in touch. One person I interviewed in 1978 sends me a card every year during the holiday season. I know, of course, that it's his way of saying, "Remember me." Still, I'm flattered that he considers me a valuable long-term professional contact.

In the larger scheme of things, doing well in your career takes more than just acing your interview. Winning strategies for getting your next job involve more than just showcasing your skills as you handle interview questions. The most important strategy of all is to be a real person, honest in your dealings with others, and willing to follow your passion in your work.

Thoughts:

NOTES

Chapter 2

1. Toossi, Mitra. "Labor force projections to 2012: The graying of the U.S. workforce." *Monthly Labor Review Online*, Feb. 2004, Vol. 127, No. 2. www.bls.gov/opub/mlr/2004/02art3exc.htm

2. Chao, E. L. Opening statement prepared for delivery by U.S. Secretary of Labor Elaine L. Chao. "Preparing for the Jobs of the 21st Century." President's economic summit, Washington, D.C., Thursday, Dec. 16, 2004. www.dol.gov/_sec/media/speeches/20041216_econ-open.htm.

3. U.S. Department of Labor: Bureau of Labor Statistics. Tomorrow's jobs. www.bls.gov/oco2003.stm

4. Buckner, Stephen. Public Information Office, U.S. Department of Commerce. *U.S. Census Bureau News*, 5/10/04. Seattle residents among nation's most educated. www.census.gov/PressRelease/www/releases/archives/american_community_survey

Chapter 3

1. Green, P. C. 1999. *Building Robust Competencies: Linking Human Resource Systems to Organizational Strategies.* San Francisco: Jossey-Bass

Chapter 5

1. Green, P. C., 1999.

2. This competency model is provided with the permission of Achilles Solutions, LLC.

3. The O*NET is a powerful tool for job analysis and career guidance. It was designed to update and replace the *Dictionary of Occupational Titles* and provides extensive information about the competencies and technical proficiencies associated with different careers. To access the O*NET, go to online.onetcenter.org or to the U.S. Department of Labor website.

Chapter 6

1. The O*NET may be accessed at online.onetcenter.org or through the U.S. Department of Labor website.

Thoughts:

RESOURCES

RESOURCE A: A STRUCTURED INTERVIEW

Name of candidate: _____

Position: Telephone sales consultant

Date: _____ / _____ / _____

Name of interviewer: _____

The Competencies to be evaluated include:

1. Goal Setting and Achievement

2. Relationship Management

3. Productive Adaptation

4. Self-Management, Planning, and Organization

The Technical Proficiencies to be evaluated include:

1. Application of Sales Techniques

2. Information Processing

3. Application of Human Resources Knowledge

Recommendation: Hire or promote ____   Not hire or promote ____

Comments:_____

Competencies

Goal Setting and Achievement: Able to set realistic, challenging goals in light of economic and industry forecasts; persist to achieve goals; convert complex goals into smaller learning objectives; manage multiple details without losing overall perspective on the work to be done.

1. Tell me about a time when you set a realistic, challenging work goal. What did you do?

2. When have you been effective in using economic and industry forecasts to help you develop a realistic goal?

3. Describe a situation when you had to convert a complex goal into a series of steps to take.

4. Give me an example of how you were able to keep perspective on your goal when you faced multiple details.

Relationship Management: Able to build and maintain high rapport and warm relationships; create a reliable flow of positive and negative information; give respect to all people, regardless of their position or status; adapt one's communications style to the needs of others; develop a network of relationships with people in one's profession or industry.

1. When did you develop high rapport with a person who was different from you?

2. Describe a time when you were able to facilitate an exchange of unpleasant information.

3. Giving respect is sometimes a real challenge. When did you find it difficult to give respect to a person in a high position and what did you do?

4. When did you adapt your communications style in order to build your professional network?

Productive Adaptation: Able to rebound from rejection and conflict; treat a negative experience as a learning opportunity; respond to time pressures and interpersonal differences with problem-solving actions; respectful of others, even when under pressure; maintain problem-solving behavior despite conflict or pressure; adapt to ambiguity, shifting priorities and change without noticeable distress.

1. Describe a time when you were able to be objective even when you felt rejection.

2. Tell me about a negative experience at work which you converted to a learning opportunity.

3. When were you able to be a respectful problem solver when under pressure?

4. What have you done to remain productive in an ambiguous situation?

Self-Management, Planning, Organization: Able to direct one's own actions in the absence of supervision; reliably follow procedures and work guidelines to reach work objectives; develop plans to achieve standing and new work objectives; set daily priorities and schedule accordingly; maintain organized work space and a filing or customer management system.

1. This job will require you to spend a large amount of time on the telephone. Describe a time when you had to manage yourself in the absence of supervision.

2. When did you follow procedures even when it was inconvenient for you?

3. Describe a particular time on your last job when your plans helped you achieve a challenging goal.

4. Tell me about your approach to managing your workspace.

Technical Proficiencies

Application of Sales Techniques: Able to systematically prospect for new business with qualified leads; present products or services accurately, with clear speech; earn trust by being honest and credible; distinguish between features and benefits; use objections as an opportunity to explain benefits; ask questions to identify needs and problems; adapt efforts to persuade in light of objections or resistance; earn the right to close business.

1. Describe a time when you were systematic in developing a sales strategy for a very desirable customer.

2. Tell me about a time when you were able to earn trust by making an especially honest product presentation.

3. Give me an example of a time when you used a customer's objections to expand your sales presentation.

4. What specific things did you do to earn the right to close business with a cautious customer?

Information Processing: Able to use customer contact management software; use word processing to communicate through letters, memos, and reports; review and edit written work for grammar, punctuation, and style; maintain database and records of customer contacts; use databases to acquire customer information and develop sales plans.

1. Describe your experience with any customer contact software program.

2. Describe your skills in using a word processor to manage customer information.

3. What is your experience in working with a customer database?

4. What have you done to help build a customer database?

Application of Human Resources Knowledge: Able to apply knowledge of standard human resource information including EEO law, the ADA, interviewing, performance management and assessment; demonstrate knowledge of basic instructional design and training techniques; apply understanding of organizational climate, learning, and core competencies to training products.

1. Describe a time when you used your knowledge of EEO law, the ADA, interviewing, performance management or assessment on the job.

2. When did you use your knowledge of instructional design to solve a training problem? What did you do?

3. How have you used your knowledge of interviewing and the law to develop a defensible selection program?

4. When have you applied your understanding of core competencies to help improve organizational performance?

Thoughts:

INDEX

Thoughts:

Thoughts:

ABOUT SKILFAST® INC.

SkilFast was designed to make skill acquisition easy and deep for today's professional. This is accomplished by having well-researched, readable books that provide practical information about workplace topics.

Publications are developed in tandem with outlines, transparencies, and videos for training in business and government. The purchase of a license provides access to the training information at a fraction of the cost of traditional certification and delivery fees.

Contact SkilFast for additional information on licensing and pricing.

SkilFast
516 Tennessee Street
Memphis, TN 38103
800-579-3942
www.skilfast.com

For special orders and bulk purchases, contact National Book Network at 800-462-6420 or <u>nbnbooks.com</u>. Quantity discounts are available.

...act Paul Green:

79-3942

or e-mail pau... ...enphd.com

Get Hired! is available on video!

A training video that parallels the *Get Hired!* book is available through American Media, Inc., a Coastal Training Technologies Company. To preview or order, call 888-776-8268 or e-mail <u>ammedia.com</u>.